I
make sense?

THIS BOOK IS THE PROPERTY OF
THE KING'S SCHOOL
BOYS' DIVISION MACCLESFIELD
and is lent to the pupil whose name is last on the list below

Name	Form	Date Borrowed	Date Returned
Neil A. Ward	L6M7-	78	

No name may be crossed out or erased on this list. Names may not be written elsewhere in this book. Pupils are responsible for returning books when finished with or when they leave. Books not returned are charged at cost price.

Does God make sense?

NICK EARLE

Polymathic

Acknowledgements

I should like to express my debt to Peter Collins, of the University of Cape Town, for unstinting help and encouragement– and for advice in regard both to this form and content of the book and its manner of publication. Also to Chris Baldwin of St. Faith's Church, North Dulwich, for typing this original draft and its many corrections.

N.E.

Copyright © Nick Earle 1998

Published by Polymathic Publishing (cc)

1 Coach House Yard, Ebner Street,

London SW18 1BY

Typeset in 12 on 13.5 pt Berkeley

Printed and bound by The Rustica Press,

Ndabeni, Western Cape

D6276

ISBN 0 620 22275 1

No part of this book may be reproduced or transmitted in any form
or by any means, electronic or mechanical or by photocopying,
recording or microfilming, or any retrieval system,
without the written permission of the publisher

Contents

1. Introduction 7

2. What does 'God' mean? 11

3. Does God exist? 25

4. Can God be good? 37

5. What is faith? 47

6. Does God do anything in particular? 55

7. Can I choose what I believe? 64

8. All in the mind? 76

9. Life after death 85

10. Postscript 95

*For the staff and pupils
of
James Allen's Girls' School*

1. Introduction

I don't know what you mean by 'glory'", Alice said. Humpty Dumpty smiled contemptuously. "Of course you don't – till I tell you. I meant 'there's a nice knock-down argument for you !'"

"But 'glory' doesn't mean 'a nice knock-down argument'", Alice objected.

"When I use a word", Humpty Dumpty said, in rather a scornful tone, "it means just what I choose it to mean – neither more nor less".

"The question is", said Alice, "whether you can make words mean so many different things".

"The question is", said Humpty Dumpty, "which is to be master – that's all".

LEWIS CARROLL: *Alice through the Looking Glass*

This is not a book about religion: the postscript is not an integral part of it and has only been put in for the benefit of readers who may be interested in that topic. It is not even a book about God; I shall advance reasons for supposing that such a book cannot be written. Rather, it is a book about the *word* 'God': the use to which it is put and whether in fact it can be used in any way which makes sense. When people say they do not believe in God they very often mean us to understand no more than that they can find no *use* for the word.

And the use to which the word is put is not necessarily a trivial matter. Consider the dollar bill. On its reverse side the words appear, "In God We Trust". The people who authorised their printing – how are they using the word?

What do they expect us to feel or do when we read it? To respect their authority in some special way? To trust them not to abuse that authority by printing too many notes or condoning forgery? Or just to feel in some vague manner that we are all in this business of giving and receiving dollar bills together and ought therefore to trust each other? Governments have a long history of using 'God' for their own purposes and we should be very suspicious of any which still do so, to say nothing of other more specifically religious institutions; and especially if they are unwilling to be questioned about their use of the term "because it is so fundamental". There are enough Humpty Dumptys in the world without adding to their number.

So this book is concerned with some of the questions that should be asked before any dialogue involving 'God' is entered into; and those in particular which provide the titles for Chapters 2 – 8. In writing it. I have tried to emphasise three points. Firstly, whatever else 'God' is intended to suggest it must suggest a matter of faith. Some people, and preachers especially, give the impression that they *know* something which their hearers do not – as though merely to believe, without knowing, were somehow disreputable. But there are many things which we do not know for certain which it is nevertheless reasonable to believe. We do not know that other people see the world as we do; they *might* be alien robots or talking beasts. Sadly, they are often treated as if they were. We do not know that the future will be more or less like the past; it *may* be that in the year 2001 many things that now appear to us as blue will then appear as green and *vice versa*. And we cannot know that we have more power to choose our future than our past; it *could* be that the future being less known to us than the past just makes it easier for us to think that way. None of these things is certain but no-one is deemed irrational for believing them – and why should that not be true of belief in 'God'?

Secondly, faith itself whatever else it is, is a matter of choice. In the light of what I have just said this may seem rather an odd assertion. But the difference between faith and conduct lies in this: faith cannot be enforced. We can be compelled to *do* almost anything (in particular to say that we believe what we do not) if only for fear of the consequences of not doing do. Often we may not even know that we have been so compelled. But it is an essential characteristic of faith that we should want to believe whatever we really do believe, whatever other reasons there may be for doing so – for example, because the evidence in favour seems to be overwhelming. At any given moment there is no neutral ground between doing something and not doing it. But between believing something and not believing it there is always room for doubt.

Finally, I insist that when we use the term 'God' we ought to be speaking of how we believe things really are. Some people when they say that they believe that God exists, are really only telling us something about themselves. They occasionally enjoy feelings or intuitions which, lacking any other explanation, they attribute to 'God'. This is not the kind of use I am concerned with. If it were, I could not hope to resolve the disputes to which it would inevitably give rise. Nor am I concerned with the use of 'God' as shorthand for 'the inexpressible'. No-one can say exactly what distinguishes 'music' from 'organised sound'. Yet we believe there is a distinction and also, perhaps, that those who appreciate music most may point us in the right direction for discovering it. In rather the same way no-one can exactly distinguish 'God' from 'power to create out of nothing' but that fact need not prevent one from trying to make the distinction. And perhaps I should add that I am not concerned with that use of the word which allows a person to speak of 'a God' or 'the God'. Not because such use is necessarily impossible or self-contradictory but simply because a line has to be drawn somewhere. Many people find it difficult to believe in God because they are trying to believe in *a* God, a God of a particular kind.

One last word. This is a book for absolute beginners. It may seem odd, therefore, to draw attention to the fact that I judge the first chapter to be the hardest to see the point of. It has been placed where it is only because that is where it logically belongs. But it could have been placed right at the end and those for whom the questions raised by the chapter headings are completely new may like to read it only when they have digested the later chapters.

2. What does 'God' Mean?

Have you ever played hide-and-seek? Most people have, or at least have seen it played. You know what happens. The quarry hides while the hunter pretends to seek. The game ends when the quarry gives itself up. At the same time it expresses great satisfaction both at having eluded discovery for so long and at having been discovered in the end. There is a more developed but less interesting form of this game in which the hunter really tries to capture his quarry but I shall ignore this for the moment.

Hide-and-seek is a peculiar game for several reasons. There are no ground rules (preconditions). No necessity for a level playing field or an eight-by-eight checker board. If there are no trees or furniture to hide behind the quarry closes its eyes. Such rules as there are, are never written down; in fact the game can be played before there is any language in which to write them down. But there *are* rules, the most important being that the quarry is never found until it chooses to surrender. And there are winners but no losers.

What is more the object of the game is never stated. Most games require, as rule number one, some such statement as 'the object of the game is to score more points than your opponent' or 'the object of the game is to capture your opponent's king'. Not so with hide-and-seek. It seems that there is no object unless it be to enjoy surprising and being surprised. And to state that object would be to eliminate surprise. Nor is the game ever played for any ulterior motive: to earn money, to amuse spectators or to prove yourself. Not even for the exercise. It is played purely for its own sake.

Languages have been likened to games. They are activities engaged in by two or more players whose participation is governed by the rules of whichever language it is. The object of the game in every case is to effect a change in the beliefs, feelings or intentions of the other players. And when you know the rules you know the game.

I wrote 'languages' in the plural in the last paragraph because there are many different kinds of language just as there are many different kinds of games. If you were to see someone knocked down in a hit-and-run incident you might say that you had seen that person die: that would be a medical or scientific judgement. You might say that you had seen him killed: that would be an historical judgement. If you had watched the behaviour of the driver and knew something of his relations with the victim you might have gone on to say that the pedestrian had been murdered: a moral judgement. And if you knew a bit about his undercover activities you might even say he had been assassinated: a political judgement.

The languages of morals and politics differ from that of science because different ground rules, things taken for granted, apply. Science makes no distinction between a person and a citizen; and it distinguishes a human being from an animal only by its observed behaviour and its genes. Morality on the other hand distinguishes persons from animals by the duty that we owe to them. And political language does something similar when it distinguishes a community from a crowd. Historical language seems to straddle the other three. And the question we have to ask ourselves is, "What, if anything, does religious language do? What are its ground rules and what is the object of the game?"

It is worth pausing here to reflect that different kinds of language give rise to different kinds of truth – and different kinds of satisfaction in supposing that one knows the truth.

Mathematical language yields mathematical truth and purely intellectual satisfaction. Scientific truth yields the satisfaction of being able to predict the future; historical truth the satisfaction of understanding the present *via* the past (your own past included); and moral truth the satisfaction of knowing – or believing that you know – what you ought to do.

The language of personal relations affords the satisfaction of recognition, of knowing other people and being known by them, known but not necessarily known *about*. It has this peculiarity, too, that it uses not only words and symbols but *body-language* – gestures, looks and intonations.

Of course some truths, for example that government ought or ought not to be obeyed, will fall into more than one category, the legitimacy of any government depending both on moral and historical criteria. We have to imagine a layered jigsaw puzzle in which some of the pieces belong to more than one layer. Does religious truth, if there is such a thing, have its own layer or does it serve to connect some or all of the other layers?

Languages don't differ only in their ground rules, of course. They differ in the ways they have developed and in the strictness with which the rules of play are expected to apply. Mathematics is in some respects the most sophisticated of languages: it is to the language of science what putting is to golf – a game within a game. Yet it has one of the most recently developed sets of ground rules. Most of them have been discovered, or invented, within the last century and an half. And its rules of play, the ways in which numbers can be ordered and combined, are being extended all the time. Yet people have been *using* numbers for thousands of years without knowing many of their possibilities or even exactly what they are.

The same is true of the words we use in everyday life. If I shout, "Help", you don't need to know whether I mean, "Help is needed", "Please help me" or "If only someone would help me!" Without making any such distinctions you know what it is that I want you to do. And if you do it I have scored a point. Incidentally this is a good example of an utterance designed to change a person's beliefs, feelings and intentions all in one go.

By the same token words alone are often quite insufficient to convey what you want to convey, however 'true' their import may be. "I am here" is a statement whose truth is incontrovertible but how much of what it conveys depends upon the context and tone of voice! To someone in the darkness of a cave, trapped and believing himself to be alone, it might spell salvation (health and safety). To someone gagged, blindfold and bound but struggling to be free the same words uttered by his captor would convey a very different message. The purpose of an utterance can also be part of the utterance itself. "There will always be something to do in the garden" may be unarguable. But is it to be understood as a blessing ("You need never be bored") or as a curse ("You can never be free")? In much the same way "God created the world" may be taken as a kind of imperative, "Don't imagine that the world can be understood on its own terms" or as a statement of intent, "I am not going to regard the world's future as something that can be taken for granted".

Languages, as I have said, vary in the strictness with which the rules apply. At one end of the spectrum is mathematics which, like chess, has precise rules but which, unlike chess, you don't need to know in full before you start to play. At the other end is poetry which can seem rather like one of those children's games in which you make up the rules as you go along. Where does religious language slot in? Is it like hockey, say, a fairly precise game but with many variations? Or is it like hide-and-seek played according to strict rules but ones which are never written down?

In fact I don't think it is quite like either. But it *is* like hide-and-seek in having some very peculiar features. For example, it uses words such as 'faith', 'spirit' and 'destiny' in ways far removed from those followed in common speech. And it uses one word which has no proper place in common speech at all, namely 'God'. The other three words I shall look at later (in chapters 5, 8 and 9). For the moment let us stick with 'God'.

At once we find ourselves in difficulties. If I say, "The President of the United States is a Democrat" you know exactly what I mean. He belongs to an identifiable group, the Democratic Party. He might be a Republican but as it happens he is not. But if I say, "The President of the United States is Chief of the Armed Forces" you know that I am telling you something not about the holder of the office so much as about the office itself. The holder of the office doesn't *happen* to be Chief of the Armed Forces. To hold the office *is*, amongst other things, to hold the office of Chief of the Armed Forces. You can't be one without being the other. In other words I am telling you as much about what it is to be Chief of the Armed Forces as about what it is to be President.

Now suppose I say, "The President of the United States is male". Unless you are familiar with the American Constitution you may not know whether I am saying that he *happens* to be male or that he *must* be male. But even if the Constitution did require maleness in the President that requirement could be changed. It is no part of what the word 'President' itself implies. To that extent we could say that the President happens to be male, if in fact he does. Whereas if 'President' is taken to be synonymous with 'Chief Executive' it *must* imply 'Chief of the Armed Forces'. No country could be governed by someone who did not have control of the Armed Forces. That is in the nature of government.

Now 'God' is generally taken to stand for something necessarily changeless. (Hence the proscription of '*a* God' and '*the* God'.) He (or it) cannot be other than he is. There is no question of his happening to be anything in either of the above senses. And this has led some people to say that in this instance the holder *is* the office. Whether they are right or not, the changelessness of God has some important consequences.

First of all it implies that anything said of 'God' not only elaborates our understanding of the way that word is used; it also tells us something about that anything.

Suppose, for example, that I say, "God is wise". I don't mean to tell you just that to be the creator of all that is one must be wise, though that may be true. I also mean to tell you that wisdom is divine and therefore to be wise one must be like the creator in some respect. In other words I am stretching the use of the word 'wise'. The same people who were wise before – Solomon, Socrates etc. – will still be wise. But not just because they have a certain capacity, say for settling disputes. They are also wise because this capacity, as well as having something to do with the structure of their brains, is a kind of consequence or reflection of God's unchanging wisdom. No-one is wise in exactly the way that God is wise. But if God wasn't wise no-one would be wise at all. Nothing exists in exactly the way that God exists. But if God didn't exist nothing would exist at all.

I am no expert in the history of chess. But I suppose that there must have been a time when pawns were just pawns, used to defend or besiege pieces of greater value. They were not potential queens. Then someone thought that the role of a pawn might be enhanced and chess made a more satisfying game if a rule was introduced that when a pawn reached the eighth square it became a queen, or whatever other piece the player chose. This new rule didn't alter the fact that pawns moved across the board exactly as before. But it did give them a new dignity. And of course it changed the game profoundly.

The pieces on a chess board are like words in a language. And the rules governing when and how they move are like the rules governing the use of words. By making a new rule about 'wise' we don't alter the way the word is used in common speech. But we do alter its dignity. That is what the statement "God is wise" is doing; altering the dignity of 'wise'. It is a statement prior to the game of religious discourse which helps to define it. It is not a move within the game itself. Talk of 'God' does not give us fresh information about the world or ourselves; rather it tells us *how the world should be regarded, what its possibilities are and what is to be done about it in consequence.* Belief in God is not something to be added – stuck on, so to speak – to a view of the world already formulated. Rather it is an extra rule to be observed in formulating that view in the first place. To ask what 'God' *means* is like asking, "What is the point of enjoyment?" Enjoyment does not *get* point from anything; it gives – or adds –point to other things: food, work and conversation. In the same way 'God' does not *get* meaning from other words; it *gives* – or adds meaning to them. And notably to the word 'enjoyment.'

Now you may feel like saying that this is an outrageous way to extend the rules of language and that therefore you are not going to play this particular game. And it is quite true that religious language hijacks a lot of the terms of common speech for its own use. But before you decide to opt out completely there are two considerations which might persuade you to keep an open mind.

What we have done with the word 'wisdom' is to say that not only will it act as shorthand for the capacity to settle disputes; it will also be placed in the category, 'divine attribute'. To say that God is wise is just to say that wisdom is divine. And we already do much the same sort of thing with, for example, the word 'gravitational'. To say that the universe is gravitational is just to say that gravitation is universal. In fact it may well be that when we have said that the universe is finite, unbounded, four-dimensional, gravitational and electro-magnetic we have said all that there is to be said of the universe in general. And when we have said that God is immeasurable, eternal, creative and rational it may be that we have said all that can be said of God in general. Though of course many people think there is more to be said than that.

And this brings me to my second point. You may object to my wanting to stretch the use of the word 'wise' to allow for God. But we already stretch its use in another direction to allow for words and actions. We speak of a wise remark or a wise decision, meaning by that the sort of remark or decision that a wise person would make. What we are now being asked to do is to talk about a wise person as the sort of person God would make if he or it didn't have to take account of that person's parents in the making. In other words we are using wise people as an analogy for God just as we talk about wise decisions by analogy with the people who make them. And if we had only heard the word 'wise' applied to words and actions we could guess, more or less accurately, what it would mean when applied to people. In other words by going from events (actions or remarks) to people we are extending the use of the word wise in a certain direction; and in going from people to God we are extending it further in the same direction.

In some of the chapters that follow I consider how certain words are used of God: in chapter 3 the word 'existent'; in chapter 4 'good'; in chapter 6 'agent'. In each case the stretch is in the same direction – from things or events through persons to God. To say that persons (other minds) exist, even to say that I exist, is not quite the same as saying that our brains exist, though there may be a connection. And to say that God exists is not just like saying that persons exist. This principle is of even more importance when we come to speak of relations between persons and relations between events or things. To say that the rule of law exists in a certain place is not just like saying that a public transport system exists there or opportunity for public debate though the one may be evidence for the other. And to say that God exists may turn out to be more like saying that divine *relationships* exist than that a divine *thing* exists.

'Goodness' when attributed to God is certainly not attributed as it is to persons; nor to persons as it is to things. And the same is true of 'power' or 'agency'. But in each case the stretch of use is in the same direction. Human goodness is more like divine goodness than the goodness of an apple because it embraces preference; and human agency is more like divine agency than the agency of a chemical because it can be exercised consciously, rationally and with some knowledge of the consequences. This point is particularly important when we speak of God as 'creative' (or as 'creator' if we want to distinguish between the holder and the office). We speak of people creating works of art when, for example, they take paints out of paint-tubes and re-arrange them on a piece of canvas or paper. We call this activity 'creation' or 'origination' because although the paints have their origin somewhere else – in the tubes – the arrangement itself has its origin in the artist; or so at least it seems. God's 'creation' on the other hand is thought of as originating solely in him. That is why he is said to create 'out of nothing'. Both matter and its arrangement are thought of as the consequences of his being what he is. But in saying this we have to use the analogy of human creation because we have no experience of creation out of nothing and cannot reasonably expect to. (The nearest likeness, I suppose, would be a completely free choice – if there is such a thing. This question is discussed in Chapter 7.)

The use of analogy in speaking of God is in fact so important (wars have been fought because it has been lost sight of) that perhaps I ought to mention two more very common instances. First God is said to *rule* the world. That is, to make the rules of nature, usually called 'laws'; to make the rules of thought and hence of language; and to make the rules of right behaviour – if there are any. The extent to which God may be said to *enforce* these rules must be left to later chapters. For the moment it is the existence of the rules themselves which is the point at issue.

A ruler is usually taken to be a piece of wood or plastic with a straight edge which is meant to ensure that the tip of your pencil goes from A to B by the shortest route. Either that or else it is a monarch who by issuing and enforcing edicts ensures that his or her people go straight – that is with the least possible deviation from normal behaviour – between the cradle and the grave. I leave you to work out, in these two cases, which is the analogy for which. The point is that both are analogies for the rule of God which ensures as far as possible that the universe conforms to his design.

Secondly, God is said to be the source not just of matter and the laws which govern its behaviour, but also of *illumination* in those creatures who are capable of it, that is to say rational beings. Hence the phrase 'the light of reason'.

We all know what 'illumination' conveys in its figurative use. When you suddenly realise why a floating body must displace exactly its own weight of water your *imagination* is illuminated. You form a mental picture of the displaced water occupying the space below the water line now occupied by the floating body and a conception of the pressure of the rest of the water on either or both. And you 'see' that the pressure must be the same in both cases, namely whatever is required to keep the floating body or the displaced water in its place.

But when you realise that under the pressure of competition for limited resources those members of a species are most likely to survive that are best fitted to do so your *intellect* is illuminated. You don't need to visualise giraffes with longer necks finding pasture where those with shorter ones cannot. All you need to do is to see that "best fitted to survive" is the same as "most likely to survive" in any given conditions.

And when you realise that it is better to be deceived than to deceive because the harm done by the former is within your power to contain while the harm done by the latter is not, then your *moral sense* is illuminated. Or so most people with a developed moral sense would say.

But those who make use of religious language want to go further. They want to say of course that all three kinds of illumination are God's doing (which need not imply that they have no natural explanation); that he is the source alike of creative imagination, rational thinking and moral judgement –

much as he is the source of wisdom. Indeed wisdom can be thought of as a blend of just those three ingredients. And as before in saying this they wish to be understood as saying in rather greater detail just what the use of the word 'God' implies. But those who use religious language also want to use 'illumination' as an analogy for something else, what those who believe in it call *spiritual* illumination: the realisation not merely of scientific or moral truth but of a kind of truth which embraces both, namely that the universe owes its existence to something else – and you and I along with it. Like the rest of religious language this involves stretching the use of a word, in this case the word 'see'. It also helps to explain why no-one can understand or 'see' God. You can't illuminate the sun. (As a famous philosopher once said, "*if* you can understand it, it isn't God.")

This brings me to the last thing I want to say about religious language in general, which is that it often seems *paradoxical* and not least when its analogical nature is forgotten.

Even ordinary language can be lured into paradox. Words are often treated like labels, as a means of sorting out our impressions; the human mind is naturally inclined to classification. Without these labels the world appears chaotic. Memories present themselves unbidden; we have no means of summoning them or distinguishing them when they appear. We know that red and green apples differ but having no words for red and green we cannot tell in what they differ; still less associate that difference with, say, a difference in taste. In that sense labels bring order out of chaos. But labels bring their own problems. Suppose we want to label words themselves according to whether or not they describe themselves. We call the word 'polysyllabic' self-descriptive because it is a word of many syllables. But 'monosyllabic' is non-self-descriptive because it, too, has many syllables but describes words with only one. Now, is the word 'non-self-descriptive' itself non-self-descriptive? If it is, it isn't; and if it isn't it is! This apparent contradiction – for that's what a paradox is – arises because in our attempt to classify *all* words as one or the other, self-descriptive or non-self-descriptive, we have created two *new* words and so extended or stretched the scope of 'all'. In the very act of defining we have damaged, if not destroyed, our definition. In the same way when we form a view of this world we change the very world of which we have formed a view.

In an attempt to tidy your room you might decide to put metallic objects in one box, paper in a second and cardboard in a third. But in order to do this you are going to need cardboard boxes; and where do they go? You can use labels or boxes for other things but you can't use them for themselves. We are up against the same problem in a special form if we try to find a box for 'God'. If God is creative of all that is but is not self-creative his existence must be of a different kind from that which he creates.

* * * * *

Archimedes, the ancient Greek philosopher and scientist, is said to have remarked, "Give me a lever and I will move the world". Language is such a lever. It is what transforms the infant into a child by enabling it to get some purchase on the world instead of just responding to it. But language is not just a labelling device and certainly not a reliable one since the use of words changes over time. (Think of the word 'humour'.) Every lever needs a fulcrum, a fixed point about which to turn, something immovable which can be taken for granted. And the lever of language turns on our belief in other minds like our own, in interaction with whom we learn how to *use* words and not just 'what they mean'.

How far persons create language and how far language creates persons is a difficult question and I propose to leave further discussion of it to the last chapter. The point here is that the mere fact of language doesn't by itself guarantee the existence of other minds. It is possible, at least in theory, to build computers that can learn to speak, to register 'pain' or 'pleasure' and even to answer questions about themselves. No-one has *proved* to me that what I call a person is not in fact just such a robot. And even if someone could, I should need to be convinced that the other person's mind *seemed* to her as mine seems to me, that her pains for example really were pains and not pleasures of a peculiar kind. As it is, this is something that I take for granted. Most other people do the same.

But such an assumption is belief not knowledge. It is not impossible to doubt it even though as children our nature compels us to accept it as true. The question for us is whether such a belief is free-standing or whether, to justify it, we either need or can gain support from a belief in God which might prevent us from treating persons as no more than thinking and feeling machines and allow us to regard them as having a unique dignity.

No lever can give you any purchase on the fulcrum upon which it turns. That is why the language of mind, as opposed to brain, never quite fulfils its promise. Archimedes' saying leaves us asking, "Can I ever get the lever of language under other people's minds? Can I ever understand – stand under my own mind even, without assuming something more?" The nature of that 'more' and what it might mean to say that it exists is what we turn to now.

But we must not expect this 'more' to be 'more of the same'. Just as religious language is not just the same as scientific language but more of it, nor divine wisdom the same as human wisdom but more of it, so belief in God will not be the same kind of belief as belief in the existence of other minds but more of it. And this is what we should expect if we are stretching the use of the word 'belief'. After all, belief in the existence of persons, other minds, is not just the same as belief in the real existence of sticks and stones. Even sticks and stones require some belief: there just might be nothing at all in the universe except my own sensations. And if we have to stretch 'belief' to take account of persons why not stretch it a bit further?

3. Does God exist?

Two people, A and B, are engaged in dialogue:
A: Do you believe in God?
B: No.
A: What sort of God don't you believe in?
B: Any sort.
A: You mean you have considered all the possibilities?
B: Yes.

This dialogue seems unsatisfactory because A ends up by offering a challenge to B on the basis of B's answers. Yet this challenge, to B, seems no challenge at all. Most arguments about God's existence are like this. The contenders are at cross-purposes because neither the word 'God' nor the word 'exists' suggests the same thing to both. So let's begin by looking at each of these words more closely. And first the word 'exists'. Here are four instances of its use or the use of the equivalent 'is'.

1. *No largest prime number exists.* This takes certain facts about numbers for granted. Numbers are arranged in succession; every number has a successor; no two numbers have the same successor and so on. On this basis it is not difficult to show that identifying any particular prime number as the greatest leads to a contradiction. (A prime number, by the way, is a number which is divisible by no number except itself and one.) Identify any prime number for me and I can show you how to identify a larger one. The

idea of a largest prime number is inconsistent with the whole idea of number. In some such way, it may be suggested, the whole notion of God is self-contradictory.

2. *There are no unicorns in England.* The facts we take for granted here are of quite a different kind. For example, that England can be divided into counties and that in each county there are people competent to identify the wild-life it contains. What the statement tells us is that if all these people were asked to identify within their own county an animal having all the characteristics of a horse together with a horn in its forehead they could not do so. In the same way, it is said, no amount of experience – our own or anybody else's – could identify God, that is locate him in time and space.

3. *No confidence exists between A and B.* This is harder to demonstrate unless we can agree as to what kind of facts would decide the matter one way or the other. We might agree, for example, that if the two people in question never spoke to one another despite being given ample opportunity to do so this would clinch the matter. But then what is ample? One or other of them might die with the matter still in doubt. What sort of criterion, it is asked, could ever establish the existence of God? And how much time must be allowed?

4. *There is no such thing as freedom of choice.* This is a harder question still. Partly, again, because it is not obvious what freedom of choice implies. But partly, too, because whatever it implies it seems that some of the evidence can only be obtained from my own brain and it is not entirely clear either to me or anyone else what is going on there. In the same sort of way if it is said that faith somehow proves the existence of God – because only God could account for it – then we have to establish what faith, which is clearly a mental activity of some kind, really consists of.

These examples are simply meant to suggest that how we set

about demonstrating the existence or non-existence of God (or anything else) is going to depend a good deal on what sort of existence we assign to him or it. The kind of search you might undertake in pursuit of a largest prime number is going to be quite different from the kind of search you would make in pursuit of an unicorn – or an instance of free choice. And similarly with any proofs of the contrary.

The nineteenth-century atheist, Charles Bradlaugh, used to astonish his audiences by beginning a lecture with the words, "I will give God sixty seconds to strike me dead!" and then producing a watch and laying it on the table while the seconds ticked by. Such a 'proof', supposedly of the fact that God does not exist, suggests some kind of magical power to be manipulated at will. This is a starting point no better than that of many so-called miracles and answers to prayer which are sometimes paraded for the opposite purpose. Only slightly better is the insistence that there must be some one identifiable event which, if it occurred, would finally show or have shown that God does or does not exist.

What most people look for and philosophers have sought to supply is a demonstration along the lines of either the first or last of those suggested above. In other words, attempts have been made to show either that the existence of God is self-contradictory or self-evident or else that it is necessarily undecideable.

Either route involves some sort of prior understanding of 'God' and arguments derived either from what that understanding itself entails or from some incontrovertible facts about the world for which God is held to be responsible. I am going to look briefly at four such 'proofs'. But the reader should be warned that none are conclusive and, more importantly, that even if they were they would deliver 'Gods' of widely differing kinds, none of them the simple equivalent of 'creator'. And it is as creator that Western man has generally regarded God.

The first proof, so-called, takes as its starting point the question, "Why does anything exist at all?" We all know why particular things exist: a pain in my finger because I put it too near the fire; my finger and the rest of my body because of my parents; my mind, in part at least, because of the way I have been brought up. And these 'becauses' refer to something earlier in time. I put my finger near the fire and *then* I felt the pain. My mother conceived me and *then* my body grew. My teachers taught me the virtue of courage and *then* I learnt to control my fear – and so on. Cause precedes effect. And if we care to trace the chain of cause and effect backwards in time we shall eventually reach the Big Bang – if there was one. But it is meaningless to ask what caused the Big Bang if there was, by definition, nothing before it. It is like asking what is north of the North Pole. If we ask why the Big Bang "happened" we shall be forced to use the word 'why' in a rather different way; more akin perhaps to asking why Mozart composed his Requiem. In such a case the cause, if there is one, is of a kind quite unlike the effect and may not be adjacent to it (at least in time) at all.

But perhaps there was no Big Bang. Perhaps the universe has been going on, and will go on, for ever. If so, that fact itself requires some explanation. Why should things 'go on'? A more refined form of the argument seeks to demonstrate not just a creator but a *sustainer* of the universe – that without which any kind of existence *in time* would be impossible. If we leave that aside for the moment we shall need to look not so much for causes which explain events in terms of earlier events as those which explain ideas in terms of prior ideas.

In your locality there is probably a public library. What accounts for it? A local authority may have commissioned it or a local worthy may have put up the money, but I don't mean that. I mean why are there libraries at all? The answer surely is to house books. Libraries presuppose books. No books, no libraries. And books presuppose authors. But what do authors presuppose? Some kind of creative instinct perhaps; or, since we want to avoid a reference to evolution which will take us back into the cause-effect chain, something which for lack of a better term we call creativity. But what does that presuppose? What accounts for creativity? (And remember, I am not looking for an answer relating to the structure of the brain.) If by creativity I mean precisely the power to account for something – an author, being responsible for his book, can be called to account for it – then the question begins to look very like the one with which the last chapter ended. The argument which seeks to establish God as a First Cause runs into the same trouble as every other attempt to put a name to God; it is an attempt to get the lever under the fulcrum.

A second, and most people would say an even less successful, argument tries to turn the first on its head by taking the word 'why?' to mean not 'from what cause?' but 'to what end?' Everything in the world, it is argued, seems to serve a purpose – or at least to be part of a pattern. Rain water slakes our thirst and washes away our sewage. It also nourishes plants which feed animals which draw our ploughs. The so-called 'boundary conditions' of the universe are just right for the eventual emergence of life. It is quite possible, the argument continues, to conceive of a universe which is entirely chaotic and in which no progress, no purposeful change, ever takes place at all. But the universe in fact is not like that. Why not? The answer suggests itself that the universe is the product of design – and design presupposes a designer.

The objections to this argument are substantial. Why one designer? What, at the end of the day, is the universe designed to *do*? That the conditions are right for the evolution of *homo sapiens* is of course undeniable; *homo sapiens* cannot reach any other conclusion since if they were not right he could not reach any conclusion at all. Again, is not the whole notion of design a mere projection on to the external, non-human world of something which rational beings find – or think they find – within themselves, namely the capacity to deliberate and form intentions? Something which compels them to ask when they see two cars in collision, "Was it or was it not an accident?" That very dilemma, either accident or design but not both, can only be posed by rational beings. It is not inherent in the event to which it refers in the same way, for example, as the contrast between regular and random. The collisions between vehicles over a period of years at a given 'black spot' may be regularly or randomly distributed over time and there can be no disagreement about it if enough such collisions occur. But there can be plenty of room for dispute about whether they were accidental or not. We don't call the dripping of water from an icicle purposeful because the drops travel in the same direction at regular intervals like blows from an hammer. Nor do we classify the falling of leaves from a tree as accidental because they drop from different branches at random times. And where there might *seem* to be purpose, in the behaviour of living things, we now have an explanation, in the theory of evolution, of which the randomness of variation is an essential part.

Of course if this argument, the so-called Argument from Design, could be made to stick it would enormously expand the meaning we could attach to the word 'God': he would have to be considered not merely a creator but a creator with a purpose, whether good or bad. But since Darwin wrote his *Origin of Species* there have been a diminishing number who believe it can.

A more promising argument, at first sight, is that from morality. In fact there are really two arguments here: the first from moral awareness, the second from the appearance of moral order.

Why do people describe one another's behaviour as good or bad? What do they mean when they justify their own actions as 'right' and condemn others' as 'wrong'? Has the word 'ought' got a definite and, more importantly, a fixed use?

It is generally accepted that the genuinely amoral person,

one to whom the word 'right' conveys no more meaning than the word 'loud' to a man born deaf, is defective. In one essential area of human life, the making of conscious choices, he is irremediably handicapped. Speech is not essential to a rational being but it is one of his most distinctive characteristics. In the same way the capacity for informed moral judgement, as opposed to mere taste or preference, is regarded by those who advance this argument as equally significant.

But why? How are we to account for this almost universal human trait? The simplest explanation would be in terms of some kind of natural or social selection. Societies are most likely to achieve cohesion and therefore to survive where parental or other authority teaches socially acceptable behaviour to those in its care in such a way that the rising generation comes to believe in the social code not as mere convention but as an unalterable law of 'morality' – the way things simply *are*.

The trouble with this account is that it equates moral consciousness with awareness of what is and is not socially acceptable; 'ought' is equated with 'owed to society' and the distinction between morality and convention disappears. In such circumstances it can never be *right,* rather than merely gratifying, to challenge convention; and no moral *progress,* as opposed to mere change, can ever be possible.

The argument from moral order tries to get round this difficulty. Experience, it is claimed, suggests that there is a central core of moral principle, progressively realised by all rational beings as they grow in rationality, despite circumstances which allow of its occasional modification. (The duty of caring for parents in their old age, for example, is played down in climates so harsh as to make adult self-sufficiency virtually imperative.) This central core includes such precepts as: speech and action should be consistent; killing other humans for sport is impermissible; children should not be exploited – and so on.

Something tells us that health, security, justice, liberty and happiness are 'goods'. And that sickness, uncertainty, inequality and misery are 'evils'. But in doing so it reminds us that what *looks* like a statement, 'health is good', is in fact a *commendation*, an utterance which authorises a moral judgement, "You ought to take care of your health." Further, that such 'oughts' must have a greater authority than mere personal preference – "I like this book so you ought to read it, but of course your taste may differ from mine." They must have an authority, greater even than a majority preference – "Eight out of ten cats prefer this pet-food so you ought to buy it for your cat, but of course the same eight may prefer something different next week."

Efforts to establish such authority are many and various. Perhaps all goods can be referred to happiness? If you want happiness, whether for yourself or others then you ought to be just, truthful and honest because only so will you make yourself and others happy. But ought you not to be truthful whether or not it makes other people happy? And in any case if you do decide to speak the truth can you be sure of the consequences? Anyhow, what exactly is this self-evident good called happiness? Why must one recommend it? Because it is an end in itself? But so is fun and fun can be harmful. The condition proper to humanity, then? That answer only introduces another moral category, propriety, and we are back where we started.

If a morality is sought based on the authority of reason alone the most plausible contender seems to be 'Do as you would be done by'. It is unreasonable, for example, to expect others to treat us as their equals if we do not treat them as ours. Unfortunately such a morality offers us no guidance in regard to questions about euthanasia, animal welfare, the treatment of criminals or the conservation of the planet.

The issue here is really whether reason alone can produce an answer to the question: what is it to say that something is good? When an accused person comes up for judgement evidence is entered and arguments are adduced as to the credibility, coherence and persuasiveness of such evidence. The judge then delivers a verdict, innocent or guilty. And if guilty a sentence, two years' hard labour. But how does he get from one to the other? He may cite other sentences in similar cases. He may quote generally accepted guidelines. But sooner or later he must introduce some moral principle, if only that such guidelines *are to be followed*. He may say that crime *deserves* to be punished; that society has a *right* to protection; that people *ought* to be deterred from committing similar crimes. And it is just such principles that are being commended when we say that justice *ought to be done*. Again, we are back to square one.

Argument normally leads one from premiss to conclusion; principle from facts to appropriate response. 'X is a Cretan' takes me from 'All Cretans are liars' to 'X is a liar'. 'Lying is punishable' takes me from 'X is a liar' to 'X ought to be punished'. But the conclusions in the two cases are of a different order. And *so are the warrants for reaching them*. Can either argument or experience or a combination of the two ever take us from fact to principle: from what is to what ought to be?

I shall have more to say of goodness in the next chapter and again in Chapter 7. All I wish to say here is that those who see in morality an argument for the existence of a Supreme Good hope to answer the question, "How do I pass from 'is' to 'ought'?" in the shortest possible way. Namely by saying that if there is a God-with-a-purpose, however little power he may have to *effect* his purpose, then that purpose, however disclosed and whether indeed it is disclosed or not, is the warrant for our moral judgements and the only possible one. And our first duty must be to try to discover it.

Now all these arguments – from cause and effect, from apparent design and from morality – share one important feature: they all use language taken from human affairs. Nobody has ever seen a cause. In fact it is difficult to say precisely what the word means. If the cause always precedes the effect does the end of the cause coincide exactly with the beginning of the effect? If not, surely another event between them could prevent the cause having its effect? If the circuit has fused, my throwing the switch wouldn't in fact cause the light to go on – which suggests that it isn't in fact the cause. But if so, how much of what precedes the effect *is* cause? The whole history of the universe up to that point? That seems as satisfactory an answer as any. For the light to go on there must have been a bulb, a circuit, a switch, me – which means all my previous history – and so back. Isn't it really the case that we derive the whole idea of cause from the fact that we humans can, apparently, cause things to happen? We decide to lift the knife from the table and lo! it happens. And even if this isn't so it is certainly a fact that science can describe all non-human affairs without reference to cause at all: the only concept needed is that of regularity – rules, in other words. Consider the case of two equal stars circling round their common centre of gravity in otherwise empty space. Are there any 'causes' at work?

The same is even more obviously true of purpose. Purpose presupposes consciousness. The acorn can have a purpose – that of producing another oak-tree – only in a mind that can foresee that it will in fact do so. It seems to us that we can produce the next generation of humans 'on purpose' so it seems appropriate to apply the same term to an acorn's production of an oak. Design, purpose or whatever you choose to call it, is just the name *we* give to the in-built instinct towards learning by trial and error which is shared by all sentient beings and perhaps some life-forms more primitive.

Happiness, if that is the end of morality, doesn't pretend to be anything but a man-shaped term. By morality we mean human morality and by happiness human happiness. This remains true even though human beings may have entirely different ideas of what their happiness would consist in if they were ever to become truly happy – or their virtue if they were to become virtuous.

The so-called ontological argument tries to avoid such terms.

It is more like an argument to prove that numbers exist, if in fact they do. It attempts to define God without reference to any human experience and to show that a being so defined not only can but must exist.

Earlier on I suggested a number of different kinds of being – the being of number, being in time-and-space, being in relationship. What kind of being can be attributed to God? To this question the suggested answer is, "the being of perfection or completeness." "That than which nothing greater can be conceived" was the definition advanced by the first proponent of this argument. And although greatness takes many forms we can see what he was getting at. If there be such a thing as knowledge then knowledge of everything must be the greatest form of it. If power, then omnipotence. If goodness then the absence of all defect. And so on. But, the argument goes on, real knowledge is more perfect ('greater') than imagined knowledge; real power than imagined power; real goodness than imagined goodness. Therefore any being which combines all perfections must have this quality, too, that its being is real and not an existence merely in the mind.

I have stated the argument in a very simple form because I am not chiefly concerned with the question of whether it is valid or not or what this 'reality' is that is not 'merely in the mind'. Obviously it is not a reality external to the mind in the same way that objects of sense are external to the brain. It is the question of exactly what is meant by greatness that interests me. Can all the supposed perfections be combined? Can omniscience be combined with omnipotence since no-one can do what he knows he will not do? Can perfect justice be combined with perfect mercy? Unless we assume that the perfections *can* be combined we shall have to put them in some sort of order and allow only so much of perfection number two as is consistent with perfection number one and so on down the list.

This is what modern defenders of this argument are inclined

to do. They select as the first perfection the quality of necessary being. By this is meant that such being owes its existence to nothing else; it is neither brought into existence by anything else nor taken out of it. Everything in time and space, by contrast, owes its existence to something else and the question is left unanswered whether the sum total of all such existences owes its existence to anything or not.

The main question which this argument raises, therefore, is this: can anything be said to exist such that its non-existence would be impossible, self-contradictory or meaningless? Is there anything that must always be and have been? It does not seem absurd to suppose that the physical universe might never have existed. But would this mean that what we understand by 'truth' did not exist? Both 'yes' and 'no' seem unsatisfactory answers. 'No' because it would still be *true* that there was no physical universe; 'yes' because it is hard to see what *else* would be true. The notion that nothing might exist at all in any sense is perplexing, and it is this perplexity which the argument seeks to exploit.

Its great strength of course is precisely that it takes little or no account of the evidence of our senses, even our moral sense; and it does seem to meet a need, rather as number does. Whether numbers 'exist' or not it seems that we cannot do without them. Now that we have invented (or discovered) them it is as though we had no choice but to do so. Perhaps the same is true of God? If so, is creativity one of his perfections? And if it is, how much of that can be combined with necessary being on the one hand and moral perfection on the other?

One of the objects of the religious language game may be to find out whether unqualified creativity (power, if you prefer it) can coexist with unqualified goodness. And then to decide whether such a combination must exist and, if not, whether the world offers any evidence that, as a matter of fact, it does.

4. Can God be good?

"If I were ever to encounter the Almighty", remarked the atheist "I would show him a cancerous bone and say, 'Explain that!'"

What assumptions about 'the Almighty' underlie this remark? And what kind of explanation did the atheist think himself entitled to? Clearly his demand (it is really a question: "what explanation can be offered?") is addressed to someone or something presumed answerable for the way things are. He can answer and ought to answer. What kind of answer is required?

One answer would be in terms of the cause of cancer. And this would certainly be worth having since until we know its cause we can take no steps to prevent it. Such an answer would be within the competence of an omniscient creator whether almighty or not. If a 'First Cause' God is deemed to know, in its entirety, of what it is the first cause, such a God could answer. Whether he ought to is another question.

But the remark suggests that something more is wanted: an answer in terms of a purpose to be served. A Designer God might be able to meet that case. But an answer, which is certainly possible, in terms of the cancer-controlling gene or genes and their capacity to reproduce themselves- an answer, that is to say, in terms of mere survival – would not, I think, satisfy the questioner. He is looking for, and failing to find, a *moral* purpose: something which will justify what seems to him a moral evil. He is postulating, and then disproving, a moral God. One, moreover, who is not just the source of morality for all other rational beings but also, if that makes sense, the source of his own.

But does it make sense? Or is there a morality, not of God's making, by which God may be judged? This is one of the oldest dilemmas which those who have thought about goodness at all have had to face. It occurs first in one of Plato's dialogues in the form: "Is that holy which is loved by the gods – or is it loved by the gods because it is holy?" (It appears in a rather different form in one of the most searching books in the Bible – the Book of Job.) I don't think there is much doubt that the atheist would choose the latter alternative.

This dilemma does not arise if 'God' means no more than a First Cause, a Designer working perhaps with intractable material – or even a Source of Morality with no power in the world. It is relevant only to that which is fully responsible for the universe in its entirety; that which for lack of a better word we call creator, and which is presumed to be in some sense both omnipotent and good. Even then I am not sure that the dilemma is quite as stark as it appears – if only because 'good' has such a wide range of use.

All the same, let's take a look at each option. And first that God is good, just as he is wise, because that is part of what is meant by 'God'; that 'being good' means sharing, in some degree, in something that only God possesses in its entirety – rather as an object is visible because it reflects some light. To this hypothesis two objections can be made. First, that in that case it makes no sense to *praise* God; and second that it requires us to believe that anything might be good for all we know. Things can reflect light which is invisible to us.

But the word 'praise' can be used in two different ways. We praise Isaac Newton for his demonstrations of the law of gravity – the consequences, that is to say, of the so-called 'inverse square' law. But we do not praise him in the same way that we praise a schoolboy for getting his sums right. In the second case we knew the answers all along and the schoolboy did well because he reached our answers. In the case of Isaac Newton our admiration is reserved for a disclosure which, had he not made it, we should not have been aware of at all. In the same way people praise God not because he has created a world which comes up to their expectations or demands; they praise him for having created a world at all.

The second objection, that anything might be good or bad for all we know, must be allowed. It may be that alcohol is an unmitigated evil or that responsibility for the future requires the systematic practice of selective breeding. It may be that "Love your enemies" is so much pious nonsense.

It may even be that God wants us to wear odd socks or no socks at all; this only seems unlikely if we believe rationality to be part of what is meant by 'God' as well as goodness. We cannot be sure. But it has to be said that as a matter of historical fact many if not most of our moral judgements – that cancer is an evil to be eliminated as soon as possible for example, or that all men and women are born equal – have been derived from what people have believed of God, namely that he wills health and justice, and not the other way round. The belief that God is rational is much older than the modern belief in the power of reason.

Let us look at the second possibility all the same: that we do have an independent authority for our moral judgements – reason, experience of what works, general agreement or a combination of all three. And that we expect God to be subject to the same authority. Can a case still be made for a good creator? If so and we want to avoid saying that God happens to be good we shall have to do for 'good' what we did for 'wise' in Chapter 2 and stretch its use.

On the face of it this shouldn't be too difficult; 'good' is a fairly elastic word. Compare it with the word 'yellow' for instance. If I show you a caterpillar, a tomato and a postage stamp and tell you that they are all yellow you won't have much difficulty in telling me, when I show you a bicycle, in deciding whether or not that is yellow too. But if I tell you that the caterpillar is good (healthy); that the tomato is good (firm and ripe); and that the stamp is good (unfranked and in date) it will not help you in the least in deciding whether or not the bicycle is good (roadworthy and reliable). The difficulty arises because in these contexts the word 'good' implies good *for* something: producing a butterfly, making a meal or sending a letter. But when we turn to more sophisticated uses of the word and speak, say, of a good book, a good action or a good person it is not so clear what we mean. What is a good book good *for*? It might not amuse or edify anyone; it might not even be read at all, yet still be a good book. And what about a good person? He or she is not so much good *for* something as good *at* something – reconciling differences, setting an example, bringing up children – or just living.

Now it seems absurd to say of a creator that he is or is not good *for* something – unless in the context of creation being good for and being good at are one and the same thing. (You could say, I suppose, that Shakespeare was both good for writing plays and good at it, but the latter use is surely more natural.) What most people mean when they suggest that God, if he exists, is not good is that he is not good at creating a world: that a better world – i.e. one without cancer and other evils – could have been created. But could it? Are we not in danger of making the same mistake as the man who tried to give spelling lessons to the inventor of the alphabet?

If the world is to be rated good or bad the first thing we have to decide is whether it has been created for its own sake or at least partly for the sake of something else. A poem might be written for its own sake or at any rate for the sole satisfaction of the poet. More often it is written in the hope that it will be published and will give satisfaction to others. The possibility that the universe was created for the sake of something else raises large questions which I propose to defer till Chapter 8. For the moment let us leave that possibility on one side and suppose that it is created for its own sake. How, in that case, might it be better than it is?

The attempt to imagine a better world is far from new. One of the oldest of such attempts is the story of Adam and Eve in paradise. The fact that this is, or may be, no more than a story does not detract from its significance; and as some of its subtleties are often overlooked it is worth while trying to take it apart.

How did the world of Adam and Eve differ from ours? In many ways, of course. Everything they needed grew on trees so they didn't have to work for it. But the most important differences were two: they didn't have to die and they knew nothing of good and evil.

Now death itself is not generally reckoned an evil. Without it the world would soon become overpopulated; most old people quite look forward to it; and the rest of us certainly don't want them (or ourselves) to live for ever. The point of the story is that when it was decided that Adam and Eve had to die this was regarded as a *punishment*. Death is an evil, in other words, when it deprives people of something they both want and believe they have a right to. And people only think they have a right to things – life, liberty and the pursuit of happiness – when they become aware of the difference between right and wrong. Until that point is reached it is simply taken for granted that things are they way they are. It was only when Adam and Eve ceased to take things for granted and decided that they could and would *choose* between the world they enjoyed and some other that the difference between right and wrong meant anything to them at all. Before that they enjoyed no rights and suffered no wrongs. Instead they freely chose to do what was right without knowing that they did so – a freedom few of us enjoy. They were perfectly happy but they did not know that they were. (Perhaps people *are* only really happy when they are unaware of the fact.) For Adam and Eve, therefore, evil was solely the result of choice – the choice to do something other than what God allowed. The theist calls this self-will. And of course many of our evils – war, crime, over-population and politically inspired famine – are the result of just such a choice or choices.

But maybe there are evils other than those which result from the exercise of choice. If so, we shall need to know what exactly it is that constitutes evil in the world. Think again of the cancerous bone. Why do we regard this as an evil? Firstly, of course, because it causes *pain*. Could there be a world without pain? What would such a world be like? There would be no warning of impending danger: a hand placed too near the fire would simply burn. That would be inconvenient when it came to gathering food but that would not matter. Starvation would be painless and the prospect of death by starvation would not be fearful since fear is a kind of pain. Nor would it be resented – unless the right to a normal life-span were assumed. The accidental death of a friend or spouse would not be grievous and one wonders whether childbirth would be the cause of joy. A felt lack of joy, when joy is *known* to be possible, is itself a form of pain. It is hard to conceive a world which is all pleasure: no boredom, no frustration. What would be the point of attempting anything if failure to achieve it occasioned no sense of disappointment? Would anything *matter*?

Sometimes it is argued that it is not pain as such but the intensity of pain which is ill-conceived or disproportionate to its purpose. But the point at which pain gives way to unconsciousness is determined by purely biological considerations. And like every other capacity, the capacity to withstand pain while retaining consciousness has developed both in humans and animals because it confers an advantage in the struggle for survival.

Perhaps, then, it was a mistake to create a world of competition? But in a finite world there will always be limited resources and the rate of reproduction must always exceed that required for mere replacement or accident will ensure that the species becomes extinct. Competition is a *logical* necessity in a world of change and chance; and God cannot do the *logically* impossible. (Even God cannot identify a largest prime number.) But of course once that fact is understood competition can be reduced by the introduction of birth-control policies. That is the paradox of the law of The Survival of the Fittest: once you understand it, it ceases to be true – or at any rate the whole truth. Evolution seems to be necessary in order to bring into existence a species with the power of choice. But once that stage has been reached it is the way that choice is exercised that determines what happens next.

Of course pain is not the only evil associated with cancer. Part of the trouble is its *randomness* – what I described as chance a moment or two ago. Certain risks can be identified but not to the point of our being able to eliminate *all* risk. And there are plenty of illnesses where the risk-factors are quite unknown. What would a world be like without any risk at all?

Science encourages our longing for certainty about the future. And its success in prediction – from the movement of celestial bodies to the effects of genetic engineering – is naturally used to justify the faith that is placed in it. But there seem to be some built-in limits to this success. At both ends of the complexity scale, randomness appears to be part of the nature of things. We can predict, within prescribed limits, how many molecules of a given mass of radium will emit alpha-particles within a given time – but not which ones. We can predict how many people will respond to a new advertising campaign, within limits. But again not which ones. Complete predictability eludes us. And if it did not there could be no such thing as free choice. If my own future were completely known to me, surely it would not be my *future*? It would certainly not be mine to *choose*.

Finally, cancer – especially in children – is regarded as *unjust*. And it is injustice more than anything else that the atheist complains of. Along with many others he claims a right to fair, which is to say equal, treatment; seventy years of life; freedom limited only by the claims of others; and the right – again subject to the equal rights of others – to pursue his own freely chosen brand of happiness.

But from whom do people claim these rights, if not from a creator? From one another? They cannot be demanded from past generations and it is not clear that they can be accorded to future ones. If God is just then the existence of wrongs requires explanation. But if he is not cannot the same be said of the existence of rights?

Or, in demanding these rights are we merely saying that the world would be a better place if everyone was granted them? But suppose they were. How could such rights be guaranteed? How to protect them from infringement by murderers, extortioners and thieves? It is one thing to make people free and equal; it is quite another to keep them so. Once grant freedom of choice and it seems that injustice and randomness inevitably follow. And with them at least some degree of pain. If we think of good and evil rather as we think of heat and cold so that evil is simply lack of good as cold is lack of heat, we might argue that there must be some disparity of goodness between one situation and another just as some parts of the universe must be hotter than others for anything to happen at all. If every moment of every day were equally pleasant, equally fair and equally predictable for everyone everywhere what motive would anyone have for doing anything? There would certainly be no grounds for *commending* anything – done or to be done. In such a world the question 'Can God be good?' not only would not but *could* not be asked. (The metaphor of heat and cold may also help to explain why evil is sometimes thought of as something positive. People speak of the power of evil much as they speak of the effect of cold – "the cold got into me" – whereas what happened in fact was that the heat got out of me. It is significant, surely, that this is just the metaphor we use when we categorise 'good?' human relations as 'warm' or 'bad' ones as 'cold'.)

The world appears to be capable of at least two descriptions, viewed from a moral standpoint. There is Milton's description of it as Paradise Lost. And there is Darwin's – as Chaos on its way to Order. No matter which interpretation we choose – and it may be that they are not incompatible – it seems that the only short cut to our destination, whether Paradise Regained or Complete Predictability, is by the overriding of our free-will. To reach either destination it seems that if God has any power at all he must guide his creatures inexorably away from situations of physical or moral danger and towards unselfconscious obedience to his will. As soon as choice is perceived *as* choice – as soon, that is to say, as the self perceives itself as a potential chooser – there must be the possibility of a wrong choice: the choice, namely, to follow whatever course of individual or social competitiveness which natural instinct, reinforced by creative imagination, may suggest.

So much for the possibility that a world capable of change might have been created better than it is: that there *is* a calculus of good and evil not of God's making and that the operation of that calculus shows the world to be defective. For my own part, I am not convinced that the apparent dilemma – either God rational but less than competent or God competent but less than rational – is quite as stark as at first sight it appears. I doubt whether our knowledge of good and evil is quite as assured as we are tempted to suppose. Not, I mean, our knowledge that there is a difference, but that we know exactly which is which. Yet if I had to choose between the two horns of this dilemma I think I would rather be impaled upon the first.

Many people, perhaps a majority, are conceived in ignorance. They are born in squalor, they live in misery and the die in despair. Yet few of them, I suspect, *want* to die – certainly not the younger ones. If being at all is a kind of goodness, since non-being is worse; if any world is better than no world at all; if God by the mere fact of his creation must be good in some degree, then the full extent of his goodness, if measurable at all, is not to be measured just by what is, nor even by what has been, but also by *what may yet be*. Divine goodness must encompass not only divine power but divine patience.

But of course this is a matter of faith. The faith, that is to say, that creativity, rationality and goodness are compatible and that they do in fact co-exist in God. The depth and strength of such a faith in someone who claims to have embraced it will of course be measured by that person's lack of anxiety, self-pity and complaint. It will not prevent such a person's *deploring* cancer, the weakness of his fellows or his own failings. But it will prevent him from *resenting* them.

5. What is faith?

People believe all sorts of things – or so they say. That Julius Caesar was born by means of the surgical operation that bears his name; that toadstools are poisonous; that the sun will rise tomorrow. The first is believed on the testimony of historians; the second on that of scientists; and the last on one's own experience, a testimony which many find it impossible to doubt.

What does it mean to believe – and what constitutes good ground for doing so? Suppose you have been offered a job which involves travelling to work either by bus or train. The bus journey is long and inconvenient, the service unreliable. So you decide to spend the last week of your holiday researching trains. The only feasible one is scheduled to arrive at your station at 8.00 a.m. and on five successive days you note that it arrives at 8.00 exactly, 7.59, 8.02, 7.58 and 8.01. You have studied statistics and calculate, on the normal assumptions, that the probability of the train arriving within two minutes of its scheduled time (i.e. 'punctually') is just less than eighty per cent. If you had been able to extend your observations over fifty days instead of five with the same result the probability would of course have been higher. On the evidence available to you it is more probable than not that the train will arrive punctually on Monday morning.

Over the week-end a stranger asks you whether this train is punctual and you tell him what you know but he then discloses that he has no interest in your answer, he was simply making conversation. However, a friend who asks you the same question *has* got an interest; he is going to work for the same firm. And on Monday morning he buys a ticket and arrives on the platform just before 7.58, announcing that he is going to see whether you are right. You, who are short of money, cannot afford to take this experimental view. You have chosen to act on your conclusions and have bought a season ticket. Who believes what?

The stranger, if asked, may say that he believes the train will arrive punctually. But since he is risking nothing it might be better to say simply that he thinks it likely. Your friend may believe *you*, that is to say that you are speaking the truth and that your calculations are correct. (Or, if he does not know what your evidence is and how good a statistician you are, it may just be that he knows you well enough to believe that you would not expect the train to be punctual without good grounds.) But it is still an open question with him whether in fact the train will be punctual on this occasion; he has risked no more than is necessary to find out. You, however, who have resolved to make an habit of standing on the platform at the appropriate time – to act in other words as though it were not merely likely but certain that the train will be punctual – can say that you believe in the train's punctuality as a regular thing; and most people are convinced that you do so believe because of the way you behave.

But *do* you believe it? Can anyone be sure how you really feel about the matter? Unless you feel at ease with yourself in making your resolution – to speak, to think and to act as though the train were always going to be punctual – can you be rightly said to believe? Does not something depend on the *strength* of your resolution? You might, for example, feel quite at ease buying a weekly or even a monthly ticket, but not a yearly one. You might feel quite at ease in saying that you believed the train would be punctual but not in acting as if it would. And would not the strength of your resolution be affected by the frequency with which the train was in fact punctual once the resolution had been made? Even in a simple case like this the question is not just "Do I or do I not believe?" but "How strongly do I believe? How much am I prepared to put at risk – my reputation only or my money also – and for how long?" One of the main differences between belief and knowledge – always assuming that there is such a thing as knowledge – is that we cannot strongly know.

And there are other factors that may incline you to buy a ticket besides your observations of the train itself. You may believe for example that the scheduling of trains is the responsibility of the railway company. Estimating the time of arrival of a railway train is not exactly like estimating that of a monsoon or the first cuckoo. There may be observations that you can make in both those cases which will enable you to predict the time of the event with some accuracy but the fact that the monsoon or the cuckoo *ought* to arrive at a certain time will not be one of them. (Though it is quite surprising how often people speak as though it was.) Consciously or unconsciously, the fact that the company has undertaken to do its best to ensure punctuality will influence both your decision to buy a season ticket in the first place and your decision whether or not, with the benefit of experience, to renew it when the time comes. In other words you will be influenced by how far you choose to *trust* the company.

I have chosen this example because it illustrates the connection between knowledge of probability, belief and trust in a fairly simple way. Belief differs from knowledge of probability by virtue of its interest in the proposition believed; trust from belief by its willingness to make that interest habitual. When we come to consider belief in God and the facts which lead people to say that they believe, or act as though they did, things are not going to be so simple. Before we do that it might be a good idea to look at one or two rather closer analogies to such belief or, as it is more usually called, faith.

And first, faith in our experience of the natural world. By

this I mean what our senses convey to us of everything except human nature itself. How might the atheist of the last chapter have answered the challenge put to him there: "Are you content to regard the onset of cancer as a random event?" If he were a scientist he might well reply, "No. Scientists have already identified some areas of risk and some forms of treatment. On the basis of past experience we are entitled to believe that by patient experiment and rigorous analysis we can discover the cause, and hence the cure, of cancer. And I do believe it."

Such a reply expresses faith in the natural order: that every effect has a cause; that the relations between cause and effect are regular; and that every regularity of this kind is in principle discoverable. But it also expresses a faith in *human* nature or, more accurately, in human persistence in its determination to discover every regularity.

Another kind of faith in human nature is expressed by the political idealist who says, "All men and women are born equal, that is to say of equal worth; all therefore should be given equal consideration and equal liberty to give effect to their aspirations so long as, by doing so, they do not restrict the equal liberty of others". Here the faith expressed is not so much in what human beings will do as in what they *ought* to do. But there is an unspoken assumption that the majority will in fact value liberty and the consideration others give to them above all else – and that these two values can and will be reconciled.

My reason for drawing attention to these faiths is not so much to examine the grounds on which they are held; you may like to think about those for yourself. But to point out that millions do in fact live by such faiths – or say they do – without in fact examining their reasons for doing so. And of course the same is true of faith in God. Notice, by the way, that the 'reasons' for embracing a faith are of two kinds: the evidence marshalled in favour of its probability and the motives which incline a person to speak and act as though that probability were a certainty. Where evidence for it is incoherent or unsubstantiated we speak of faith as unreasonable; where its motives are inconsistent or unacknowledged as irrational.

Perhaps the best – and certainly the most popular – analogy for faith in God is the trust which is commonly placed in money. By faith in money I don't mean just the belief that "money can do anything" or that "every man has his price". But that money will in fact do what it ought to do – what those who create it *mean* it to do.

I wonder if you can remember the amazement you felt when you were first told to push a cylindrical piece of metal across a counter or into a vending machine and at the same time express a preference for a particular type of chocolate bar. The faith in money that you began to acquire on that day had fairly good grounds. Your government had authorised the Mint to issue that coin and had taken steps to catch and punish both the forger and anyone who, within its jurisdiction, refused to accept it as legal tender. Faith in money, though you did not then realise it, was grounded in faith in government to undertake just those obligations and to resist the temptation to devalue your money by minting more than it ought. In practice you may have believed in money because other people did and you wanted to share the advantages they enjoyed by doing so. But when you looked into it you realised that the faith required was more than just faith in one another.

Faith in God as creator is, on this analogy, just faith in his government of the world which includes the making of the rules which hold it together much as secular government makes the rules which hold society together (the rules governing the use of money being among the most important). But we ask of a secular government what other purposes it has in governing beyond just keeping things going. And if we have faith in God we may ask what his purposes are, too.

A creator who creates without purpose may be an object of belief but scarcely of faith. A person without faith, in other words, may believe *that* such a creator exists but not *in* his creation. Such a person risks nothing by believing that things are as they are for no other reason than that they were made so. Though even by that he may gain something if he believes, as theists insist, that such a God, unlike the pagan gods, is rational and self-consistent. To accept, on the other hand, that God sustains the universe in being until the end of the last act, which act constitutes the purpose of the whole play, is something very different. It fits well with the notion that tomorrow's world and yesterday's world are both part of a single timeless act of creation. It suggests that God is to be found or at any rate looked for in the possibilities of each successive moment – with all that that implies for freedom of choice. And it gives reason for supposing that life is not without purpose. What ought to be will be – as no doubt the scientist and political idealist would agree. The difference in their case being that they have different understandings of what ought to be – and different reasons for believing that it will be.

What grounds there might be for faith in such a God is a question which requires a separate chapter. I will say no more here than that they involve the trustworthiness of persons as much as the truth of propositions. Indeed more so since the truth of the propositions of faith are generally commended to us in the first place by the trustworthiness of those who invite us to consider them.

But what do we mean by trustworthiness? Why trust anyone at all? And why X rather than Y? Suppose you find yourself in a foreign capital with only a small amount of currency, a map employing a strange alphabet and an address where you hope to find a friend who speaks your language. You are free in the sense that no-one is constraining you to follow any particular course of action but you know that you must surrender some of that freedom if you are to gain your end. You may ask help from passers-by; you may try to compare the signs on public transport vehicles with those on your map; you may even throw yourself on the mercy of a taxi-driver. But you have got to surrender some of your freedom to someone. The taxi-driver, if you could afford the fare, might offer the quickest and most convenient solution to your problem, but at the cost of the greatest surrender – that of your freedom of movement. In a city with a reputation for violence and anarchy that might be too big a risk to take. Asking a stranger means giving up more time than you wish and the risk of being misunderstood and having to ask several times. The bus-drivers must be fairly trustworthy or the public wouldn't use their buses. You opt for public transport with good, if not sufficient, reason. (The public might have been told to use the buses by an omnipotent dictator but in that case you would expect to see some sign of it in their faces.)

There are many situations in which you must choose whom to trust. In illness which doctor? In prosperity which bank? And your only guide may be an estimate of which is the least among several apparent evils. In fact, faith is essential to any creative act. It is just that this is most obvious in the creation of conscious relationships. You must believe that you can 'get on terms' with another person before taking the first step towards doing so.

In the last chapter we looked at the question "Can God be good?" and found it to be a very slippery one, perhaps even meaningless. It may be that a more important question is "Can God be trusted?" To trust no-one but yourself and nothing but the evidence of your senses is a practical impossibility. We were born trusting – our chances of survival would have been very slight if we had not been. But as infants we had little choice about whom to trust. Now we seem to have a great deal. What criteria are we going to adopt? Does the behaviour of other people and the course of history in general suggest some principle of choice? If God exists can he reasonably be expected to disclose his hand? In the search for God are there any promising signs?

6. Does God do anything in particular?

A recent invention is the 3-D card. On a flat surface a pattern of recurring images is displayed, usually in colour. At first sight there seems to be no meaning in the pattern. In fact it has been created by a computer analysis of the images required on the retina of each eye for a three-dimensional image to be realised in the brain. Focus the eyes on a point a certain distance *behind* the card, a point invisible to you but whose position you can imagine, and after a time you will 'see' a three-dimensional object – a hemisphere it may be, a cone or even a birthday cake. You can see what you are meant to see if you are sufficiently determined to do so. And in an important sense what you see is there. Everyone who sees the cake sees the same number of candles on it. You cannot choose what you see. There is no knowing before you see it (except perhaps to a neurologist and of course the designer of the pattern) what you will see. And no knowing how long it may take you to see it – something which depends, in part at least, on the determination you bring to the task of seeing. What is certain is that you must *choose* to see it if you are to see it at all. And your choosing to see it is likely to depend on your trust either in the designer and the instructions which accompany the card or in a friend who claims to have seen it for himself.

This chapter is about the evidence, if there is any, not merely that the world is created with a purpose but that part of that purpose at least is visible to those who choose to look for it. In other words not only that what ought to be will be, but that part of what ought to be has been disclosed in advance.

You will recall that I said in the last chapter that the belief that what ought to be will be takes many forms, not all of them religious. Those who believe in the ultimate triumph of science or rationality, for example, must base that belief on some assumption or other, if only that they have enough knowledge of scientific progress made in the past to allow them to project its course in the future.

But this assumption is not sufficient. There are two others at least that must be made. First, that the world *has* a future. And second that that future does in fact depend on the ability of the human race both to agree about what ought to be and to want it enough to ensure that it will be.

The first of these assumptions is not self-evident. The world can only come to an end once which means that there can never be enough evidence for us to calculate the probability of that event occurring at any particular moment – unless of course we introduce further assumptions about *how* it is going to end.

The second assumption is even more doubtful. There is no doubt a certain amount of agreement about what ought to be the case. Most people agree that living things ought to be healthy; rational beings ought to behave rationally and so on. But there are vast areas of human life where no such agreement is in sight. Equal status for women and men is an obvious case in point.

The scientist, someone with the kind of faith in science that I have described, has one answer to this dilemma. It is an elitist answer but not necessarily the worse for that. Trust the scientists, he says, and give them the resources they need. The democrat, of course, prefers to trust the masses, reckoning that only what they agree upon is likely to get enough backing to be put into practice.

The theist's view is different from either of the others'. What ought to be is, for him, something that cannot be understood either by the mere observation of nature or by looking into one's own mind; not even by a chain of reasoning which takes account of both. It is something disclosed. Partially and fitfully, no doubt. But inviting confidence as time goes on and as more people accept the directions of those to whom the earliest disclosures have been made.

Such disclosures, if indeed they occur, can take one of three forms. Firstly, *miracles*. Secondly, *prophetic utterances*. And thirdly, the *illumination of moral consciousness*, together with the *holiness of life* which ensues. The last category is the most difficult to identify but for that reason illustrates a point of great importance, namely that disclosure of the divine purpose is a matter of degree. Anyone can experience what he or she may describe as a moment of illumination, obtain an allegedly unique insight into the course of history or even be cured of an illness in an inexplicable way. But the long-term effects of such events will vary widely. The effect of a so-called 'conversion experience' in particular can very quickly fade. And the extent to which other people will be convinced that such events are indeed 'acts of God' will depend very much on their long-term effects. By an act of God is here meant an event which differs from others precisely in its long-term significance – the kind of future which it points to.

Every event is an act of God in one sense. If God is regarded as sustaining all things in being and determining the laws which govern the relations between events – if that's what creation out of nothing means – then of course God must be held responsible for both what we call good and what we call evil, something which many self-styled believers seem reluctant to allow. But, says the theist, it is only the end of all things which is good without qualification. Events in time are 'good' just in so far as they anticipate that end, in the way that a betrothal anticipates a marriage. Every promise fulfilled just because it is a promise and not because someone's reputation depends upon it; every truth told just because it is the truth and not to win an argument; every work of art created for art's sake and not for money or esteem is, so to speak, a miracle in miniature. Why? Because it points towards what ought to be, a state of affairs in which every event is an expression of beauty, truth or goodness and nothing else. And if any event is sufficiently unexpected by those who claim to have witnessed it and sufficiently unmistakable in its long-term significance then it will be regarded as miraculous, full stop.

But to claim that an event is *supernatural* is another thing altogether. Here the claim is not that the event is uniquely significant but that it has no natural explanation. And such a claim can only be made in the context of one's knowledge of nature at the time. A supernatural event so-called is an event not contrary to nature but to our *knowledge* of nature. And our knowledge of nature changes. Yesterday's supernatural event may be tomorrow's scientific certainty – or even today's.

Take as an example an instance of 'miraculous' healing. Can we ever be sure that such an event was in fact irregular – that it broke the rules? The answer must be "no" for at least two reasons. First, the event is now past and of necessity unrepeatable; the sick person is cured and can't be cured again. No-one can know all the circumstances. And unless we were ourselves witnesses we cannot know any of them and must trust whose who were. What compelling reason have we to do so, particularly if they are now dead?

And even if we could know the circumstances down to the last detail our knowledge of the regularities of nature may not be enough to guarantee the outcome of every possible combination of such circumstances. Furthermore, with the growth of that knowledge we may discover that what at first sight appeared irregular was not so at all. Two hundred years ago almost nothing was known of the origins of hysterical paralysis. Today we know that this condition is often the result of unacknowledged guilt. Find a way of relieving that condition

– perhaps by bringing it into consciousness – and it may well be possible to enable the dumb to speak and the lame to walk.

A cure of this kind if it took place a long time ago could well have been regarded by onlookers as supernatural. But even if it were not irregular it might well have been a miracle – because it served to disclose what nothing else could have disclosed, namely that paralytics *ought* to be healthy (their sickness is not 'God's will') and that humanity *ought* to know how to restore their health. That being so the event would not only reinforce faith in God but give grounds for faith in humanity also – even to the point of suggesting that the former may entail the latter.

Consider similarly the claims of prophetic utterance, an allegedly supernatural ability to read the signs of the times. Again, how can we be sure that this is not merely rare but positively irregular? The events to be interpreted are unrepeatable and a far-sighted view of their outcome is not necessarily beyond the scope of human intelligence and imagination. If Mozart at the age of eight was able to extend our appreciation of melody, why could not Samuel at the age of twelve have enhanced our perception of the moral order? (The story goes that, perceiving the iniquities of organised religion in Israel in the eleventh century B.C. he announced the forthcoming demise of its ruling dynasty.) The fulfilment of his prophecy suggests that people *ought* to know that the abuse of authority leads to the disintegration of society and *ought* to care enough for its long-term future to refrain from such abuse.

With the benefit of hindsight we can of course see that not all prophecy carries equal weight. The storming of the Winter Palace in St. Petersburg in 1917 was not in fact the inauguration of the workers' paradise that it was announced to be; history has proved that particular faith to be mistaken. But at the time the probabilities seemed to many intelligent people such as to warrant risking their lives in that faith – and the same is true of other faiths today. Religious faith which is distinguished by its concern for *final* outcomes cannot hope to base its whole case on prophecies fulfilled. What faith's adherents can reasonably do is to use fulfilled prophecy as evidence of the reliability of its witnesses. And trust in such witnesses – for whatever reason – has generally been necessary to faith.

Claims to be supernaturally inspired are also sometimes made for the sudden illumination of moral consciousness particularly if it is accompanied by a radical change of life-style. The person who feels morally compelled to embrace a leper or kick his addiction to drugs and whose yielding to such compulsion marks the beginning of a new lifestyle is said to have had a conversion experience. And such experience is often taken both by its subject and those who witness his conversion as an indication of what human life *ought* – and ought not – to be.

In such a case it is even harder to distinguish between the rare and the allegedly irregular. Enough is known of unconscious conflict to make it at least possible, even probable, that the event is the result of such a conflict being resolved. The addition of mystical experience – a claim, that is to say, of direct awareness of God – makes the question no easier since for the latter event we can have only the subject's testimony. Collective mystical experience which is rarer still does not significantly alter the case. And why are we to trust the subject or subjects of such experiences? The fact that Joan of Arc was prepared to go to the stake for her 'voices' only confirms the view that there is something in human nature which can prefer death to dishonour or the total loss of self-respect. Plenty of sea-captains not otherwise known for their heroic virtue have been willing to go down with their ships.

There is, however, one peculiarity of mystical experience which ought to be mentioned. The God of whom direct awareness is claimed is almost always characterised by *changelessness*; and access to such experience is said to presuppose the abandonment of interest in what is liable to change. But how can such a God bring about this abandonment – and therefore a change in the subject of the experience? How can the changeless effect change? The answer usually offered is that the mere contemplation of changelessness will suffice – rather as when a person contemplating a picture or even a geometrical figure finds that all other interest ceases. "That picture made me dizzy" implies a change in me without implying any change in the picture. The story is told of an old woman, living in a remote part of Russia, who spent many hours each week before one of the icons of Christ displayed in the local church. Her priest, puzzled by her behaviour, asked her how she spent those hours and what she hoped to gain by doing so. Her reply though strange to modern ears is nonetheless worth pondering: "I look at him and he looks at me".

But if this is indeed possible what need is there to regard the outcome, the vision of God or the hearing of his voice as in any way irregular or supernatural? Is there not in fact something lacking in a God who has to act irregularly – to suspend, so to say, his own rules, including the rules of human psychology – in order to convince his creatures of his own existence? Is not a moral or spiritual evolution, even if achieved by a different kind of mutation, just as natural as a physical or intellectual evolution? In any event what would it mean to say of such an event that it was 'caused by God'? Such a cause is precisely not a cause in any sense hitherto given to the word. At best it is simply a new form of account.

Many events seem to warrant at least two forms of account. What happened when I saw the snake? Adrenalin was released into my bloodstream *and* I felt fear. What happened when Charles Dickens wrote *Great Expectations*? Ink was deposited on paper in a systematic way *and* creative genius received expression. And both accounts are needed if justice is to be done to what has taken place. To give an alternative account of an otherwise unexplained act of healing is not to deny that such an event – call it a miracle if you like – is significant. On the contrary that is just what it is. But it is significant not because it happened but because it happened so far ahead of its time. What happened when the paralysed man walked? An irrational feeling of guilt was exposed *and* the bystanders had a glimpse of a world to come.

The new form of perception which I described at the beginning of this chapter – 3 D seeing or seeing into something – may be taken as a likeness of two world-views: the scientific and the religious. It is intended to suggest that the universe can be at one and the same time just what the scientists tell us that it is, a world of matter functioning according to fixed rules, *and* a world created in pursuit of a divine purpose. In other words to see the world as something purely material and to see it as something created, whatever that implies, involves the use of the word 'see' in two distinct senses, one literal and the other figurative and neither more valid than the other. Is it any 'truer' to say that adrenalin was discharged into my bloodstream than to say that I was frightened?

If I show you a rose what do you see? If you are a biologist you may see just the custodian of a rose's genes. If you are an artist you may see an object of beauty – a symbol, perhaps, of feminine pulchritude. But if you are a believer you will see something created and therefore *transient* – here today and gone tomorrow. And for that very reason a pointer towards that which does not change, namely its creator. The artist affirms this by capturing for *all* time a single moment *in* time.

But to see this you have to dwell on just those aspects of the rose which bring this quality of transience to mind – just as in order to see the 3-D image you must focus your attention on something which, in the literal sense of the word, you cannot see. This way of seeing the rose, like the others, becomes habitual with practice – and only so.

People don't wake up one morning and find themselves believing in God for no reason at all any more than those with political commitment or faith in science. When Charles Darwin put forward his Theory of Natural Selection he admitted that there were still obstacles to belief. The fossil record was not complete; there was at that time no theory of inheritance to explain how new variations within a species could be preserved from one generation to the next. Nor could he offer any predictions of the kind which, for example, Einstein's Theory of Relativity affords and which, if verified, would substantiate his claims. All he asked was that his theory should be accepted as a new and better interpretation of the available evidence; and for that reason something to be made the basis for further research which would, in turn, make for greater credibility. That is very much the kind of invitation which is extended by those who claim to see evidence of purposeful creation in the course of human history. And the rare but significant events which they call miracles are the clues which they offer as aids to those who are willing to undertake the necessary search. As in any treasure hunt, the confidence of those who follow the clues is increased when one clue is found to lead to another.

In practice, however, different events are claimed by different groups of people as affording the most significant clues. A calls X a 'prophet'; B rates him a 'wise man'. What appears as sanctity to one person is no more than neurotic obsession to another. The justification for the faith of the individual is very often the existence of a believing community of which he finds himself a part. The creation of that community in the first instance -its primeval faith – is for him the one indisputable miracle. "I believe in the community to which I belong because I believe God created it. I believe that God created it because I belong to it. And I belong to it because I believe in it." The argument is circular and 'God' becomes an in-house word. Can this circle – vicious or virtuous – ever be broken? If so, how does it happen?

7. Can I choose what I believe?

Imagine yourself lying in bed, fully awake, your alarm clock having woken you as you had determined it should. Unfortunately you were late to bed the night before and would like to go back to sleep. Five minutes remain to you before you have to get up if you are to catch the train that will take you to work. Not long enough for you to get more sleep but long enough for you to think about it.

What goes on in your mind? Reasons for getting up present themselves. If you do not turn up for work your boss will be angry when you next see him; perhaps your chances of promotion will be put at risk. In any case your colleagues will have to cover for you. But there are also reasons why you should not get up. You need the sleep. Today is Friday; you could easily plead a minor illness and by Monday your absence will have been almost forgotten.

Then you remember that you had promised the boss that you would get a certain piece of work completed by the end of today. That places you under an obligation. You ought to get up regardless of circumstance, whether the boss or your colleagues will be in or not. There is still a minute to run on the clock but you tell yourself that at the end of that minute you *will* get up. Then, with thirty seconds to go, a phone call informs you that because of a bomb scare your place of work will be closed all day. You thankfully relapse into sleep. Had you chosen freely? Had you chosen at all?

Freedom is a word which, like a lot of words, is best understood by contrast with its opposite – imprisonment. A man who is gagged and bound, hand and foot, is not free; he is not free to speak or move. (Of course he may be more free than he appears to be, even to himself. Houdini the escapologist appeared to other people to be bound when in fact he was not. And even you and I with patience and practice may be able to loosen some of our mental bonds, most obviously prejudice and force of habit).

Remove the gag from the man's mouth and he is able to speak. Remove his bonds but place him under house arrest and he enjoys limited freedom of movement. Remove his passport but otherwise free him from all constraint and he may hardly notice his lack of freedom. It is not a question of being either free or not free but of *how* free you are and in what respect. The same thing is true in regard to freedom of choice. Ask yourself when you are next very tired how free you are to choose to remain awake or when next you forget someone's name how free you are to choose to remember it. How much freedom did you enjoy and of what kind when you lay in bed?

First of all you were free of the necessity of an immediate decision. You had some time in which to try to make up your mind, to reason with yourself. There was time during which some of your wants, both those tending to make you stay in bed and those tending the other way, could surface, present themselves to your consciousness and perhaps have their strengths measured, the one against the other. The force of a want might be modified in the course of those five minutes by the weight of an argument for or against. You want to be popular with your colleagues and that want is strengthened by the knowledge, which it may take you some time to arrive at, of the amount of extra work which your absence will create for them. The more rational you are in your deliberations the less each want will be a matter of mere impulse and the more it will become a calculated intent. If you are a completely rational person each intention will be exactly weighted in proportion to its effects. And to the extent that you are not entirely rational but a creature of instinct or prejudice, you are not free. Nor are you entirely free of past influences which have helped to form your preferences and habits of mind. If you were you would still have the same wishes you had as an infant and no others. Was it the same 'you' then – the one who had made all the necessary calculations – who made the choice to get up? And if so was that 'you' the same person as the one who woke up four minutes earlier or had your conscious preferences changed, and 'you' along with them, as a result of this reasoning with yourself? And what if that helpful telephone call had not come through? Can you be sure that you *would* have got out of bed?

I doubt whether there is any way either you or anyone else can answer that last question with complete certainty. It may be that in similar circumstances in the past you have always done what you decided you were going to do. That makes it more likely that you are a determined person, one who when she thinks she has decided a question has in fact done so. But it does not make it certain. And in any case in what sense is this decision yours? The considerations present themselves to your mind. You do not select them and you can hardly be said to have created them. And may it not be that the calculations you made in regard to them were just those which any person as rational as you would have to have made? So perhaps what went on in your mind was what *had* to go on, given all the circumstances. Perhaps everything you think you choose to do is really the outcome of your inheritance at conception and all the experiences, good or bad, which you have enjoyed or suffered since then. Perhaps your life is only yours in the sense that it is the only one you are able to view from the inside. And the watching part of you is distinguished from the thinking and doing parts by the fact that its activity *follows* theirs and is therefore always looking back at them. On this hypothesis that part of your behaviour which appears to be completely constrained, the so-called 'knee-jerk reaction', differs from the rest of your behaviour only insofar as your reaction to circumstances by-passes that part of your brain which makes you aware of other 'possible' reactions and in so doing delays the reaction itself. There is of course a part of you which can look forward to what you may do or think in the future – your imagination. But that is not what I am trying to describe. The idea that the watching part of you, the part that looks backwards, is able to say to the rest, "Do this" or "Don't do that" may be an illusion because the decision to do it or not to do it has already been taken, if only just.

Some people, for example those who have had a near-death experience, claim that they have actually experienced this detachment of the watching self from what it watches – even to the extent of watching the preparations being made for their own death as any other observer might watch them. Such detachment, if our supposition is true, is equivalent to the loss of an illusion, to seeing things for once as they really are.

Suppose it were true then that we are nothing more than circumstances have made us; that in reality we are detached observers of our own lives though so close to them that the doing and the watching *seem* to be all one. Could we know that this was the case? First of all we should have to say that since the growth of self-knowledge is one of the things we watch there must be a kind of self-consciousness, the kind that gives rise to shame and guilt for example, which is part of what we watch and not itself part of the part that watches. That suggests an infinite regression: a self watching a self watching another self . . . and so on indefinitely.

More importantly, the very fact that we knew – or thought we knew – that our lives and everyone else's were just the result of everything that had gone on before and the only possible result (because of the laws of heredity, psychology and so forth) would entail that that 'knowledge' itself was as inevitable as everything else about us.

But would that matter? The fact that the result of an arithmetical calculation is predetermined, i.e. there is only one answer, doesn't in any way prejudge what the answer will be or alter the fact that if the calculation is done correctly it will produce the correct answer. So if in fact we had reached this knowledge – that everything, our own thinking included, was predetermined – by correct reasoning from agreed facts then it would indeed be knowledge.

More importantly still, perhaps, could we in such circumstances justly praise and blame? One of the reasons which I suggested might make you get out of bed when you did not in fact feel like it was that you had made a promise, put yourself under an obligation to finish a task by a certain time. In other words that for this reason you *ought* to go to work. Now this is a different kind of reason from the others, fear of the boss's wrath, a wish to retain your colleagues' affection and so on. None of those reasons necessarily involve any thinking on your part. Your fear of the boss, of which you may be largely unaware, may impel you to get up at once 'without thinking twice about it'; but the promise you made needs to be *remembered* ('pondered' might be a better word) if the sense of obligation which is created is to have any effect. It is important to distinguish reasons for doing something which are part of your circumstances or your own nature, i.e. direct causes, from reasons which necessitate your thinking about them if they are to become causes at all. Only a rational being, one that is to say who does not act entirely from habit or on impulse, can make a promise and thus deliberately reduce his own freedom. The promise itself may be freely made – if anything is ever done freely – but once made the person who makes it is not free.

How firmly is he bound, then? Does the making of a promise generate any impulse towards keeping it? Can we create feelings within ourselves simply by uttering the words, "I promise to do so-and-so"? And if we can are we just drawing on feelings about promises in general which are already there inside us as a result of our upbringing or have we brought into being a truly new state of affairs? When you go back to work, having broken your promises, the boss may say, "I can understand that respect for me or loyalty to your colleagues did not weigh heavily with you but I did expect that you would keep your promise". And if he does is he justified in doing so? Or is he, in saying this, merely appealing to an upbringing which you did not have? Those who argue for free choice at least in the making of a promise would argue that this does create, out of nothing, a genuinely new state of affairs, whatever the reason for the promise might be. Insincerity in making a promise does not excuse the maker from keeping it; only duress does that.

But again, does it matter for practical purposes which view we take? There is a tale of a youngster leaving a juvenile court after being convicted of shop-lifting and remarking to his father, "What's wrong with me, Dad? Is it my heredity or my upbringing?" He was certainly what we would call a determinist. But does that excuse him? Whatever his reasons for wanting to commit the offence and however slight the inhibitions which his past history may have generated he knew – or ought to have known – that society penalises shop-lifting, and as a rational being he was capable of calculating the risks. If he declined to do so that was nothing to do with his morality, unless to be irrational is to be immoral. He just found the effort of reasoning too great or the result too unpalatable. But society punished him for his shop-lifting, not for his lack of energy or taste. In other words we attach blame to the act itself, whether the breaking of a law or the breaking of a promise. And we measure the degree of the blame by the force of the circumstances whether we believe in free choice or not.

Faith is a different matter. Choosing what to believe, or even whom to believe, is unlike choosing what to do in at least two respects. First of all the result is lasting. Once an act is done the choosing is over; a fresh act will require a fresh choice. Of course many choices similarly made in similar circumstances become habitual, like always choosing to have milk in your coffee. In the same way faith by being constantly exercised becomes strong. But faith once chosen presupposes habit: choosing to believe is precisely choosing to make an habit of thinking and acting in the light of whatever it is that is to be believed. If you say to X, "I will trust you on this occasion only" you are not trusting him-as-a-person but him-in-these-circumstances. You may – indeed must – trust the taxi-driver for the duration of the journey. You needn't therefore trust him to sell you the taxi for a fair price.

There is another reason why a choice of faith is different from a choice of action. No-one else can have the same grounds as you for believing that you have indeed chosen it. Faith, whether in animal rights, spelling reform or anything else, is something internal like the effect of a promise. Indeed it *is* the effect of a promise. When you resolve to believe in God or Lenin or Liberal Democracy you are promising yourself that you will act in the appropriate way when the occasion arises. And this acting will of course include the mental acts of reminding yourself of what you profess and drawing the necessary inferences. And the sincerity as well as the strength of your resolve will be expressed in the decisions you take in any relevant situation. But until such a situation requires it no-one else will know what you believe unless you choose to tell them and even then they will probably wait until such a situation arises before deciding whether you are sincere. You may say that you believe in umbrellas but no-one else can be sure of it – until it rains.

But perhaps the most important thing about the question, "To believe or not to believe?" is that you may never be in a position where this is a live choice at all. There are of course many choices that you may never have to make. Whether to fight for your country, for example, or whether to divorce your spouse. (Though, as it happens, both these choices if they do arise may turn on what faith, if any, you have.) But both are live options in the sense that you can more or less vividly imagine what it would be like to be faced with such a choice. You can even consider what choice you might make in such circumstances and why.

With faith it is different. Although I know something about its tenets, Marx-Leninsim means nothing to me. I have no personal interest in it. I cannot imagine what it would be like to have occasion to adopt such a faith. (I can of course imagine having to pretend to do so, but that is a different case.) And the reason, I suspect, is that I have never known anyone who has adopted it well enough to know what it means to him – and therefore what it might mean to me.

It is the same with other faiths. As long as I entertain whatever faith I do, I tend to exclude, almost without thinking, the possibility of entertaining any conflicting faith. Because faith is habitual I cannot *suddenly* choose whether or not to adopt a faith as I can and must choose whether or not to greet a distant acquaintance in the street. Faith can *become* a live option but not all at once except in very rare cases – and even then appearances can very often be misleading.

But when faith does become a live option, can it be freely chosen? The freedom to choose in such a situation is not just a matter of circumstances. By saying that faith is a live option I mean that circumstances are favourable, of course. But those circumstances – the friends you know, the books you read, the arguments which both advance – can they by themselves compel you to believe or disbelieve? To put the question another way: if these influences alone cause you to change your mind does this really amount to a change of belief? Remember the difference between thinking something probable and believing it – you must have an interest in it. Remember, too, that faith involves promising yourself something. Is there not something which you, poised as you now are between belief and disbelief, must contribute to such a change of mind? Must you not *want* to believe?

Even if the answer to that questions is "yes" of course that does not mean that your choice of belief has not been made for you. It may still be the case that your change of mind was inevitable. But it is also true that when the arguments and evidence are equally balanced, so that it is equally reasonable to believe or not to believe, there is within the potential believer something – some want, I think I have to say – which tips the balance one way or the other. Nor is there anything odd about this: to live a rational life you must *want* to act on the deliverances of reason.

Wanting to do something is different from merely wishing to do it. Want implies a lack so that wanting to do something is, at least in part, *needing* to do it. We do what we want to do in order to obtain some kind of satisfaction, emotional or physical, intellectual or moral, short- or long-term. I want to do something in order to be better for having done it. If I didn't want anything, not even my next breath, I should be dead. Wishing to do something, on the other hand, may have nothing to do with need; it may be a mere whim or fancy like wishing to ride on a winged horse. This helps to explain why our wishes are generally known to us; our wants very often are not. You don't say of a person, "She doesn't know what she really wishes". An infant has no wishes at all – but it has any number of wants.

And it is to this 'wanting' factor, I suspect, that we must refer the word 'freedom' in the phrase 'freedom of choice' – at any rate when we are thinking of choice of belief. Not freedom from external pressures; on the hypothesis I am putting forward these have balanced themselves out. Not even freedom from the influence of argument; again, the arguments have, on this view, exactly cancelled one another. In this context 'freedom' means freedom from internal conflict – emotional conflict if you like – between what I want and what I ought.

For 'ought' brings its own 'want' with it. It may be a very feeble want. But if I do not want to do as I ought *at all* then I simply do not understand the word. The choice between what I want, regardless of what I ought, and what I ought, regardless of what I want, is only resolved when one outweighs the other to the extent of leaving it powerless. Only then am I completely at ease with myself in making the choice to believe or not to believe. When and only when 'I want' becomes 'I ought' or *vice versa* can I be said to choose freely or, which comes to the same thing, not to choose at all. And the choice to believe that what ought to be will be – the choice of faith – must begin, in principle at least, with a resolution of that conflict within myself in favour of what *I* ought. Until that much is done faith's expectation must remain unfulfilled. I cannot, if I am rational, look forward to a world in which men and women are left free to pursue happiness for themselves without interference and at the same time exploit my friends and neighbours.

Choice is always between things we want to do, more or less. And the act of choosing ends when, after whatever deliberation is possible to us, we do what we most want to do. Not what we most want in the short-term necessarily. The thing you may least want to do in the short term is to take a medicine which will induce vomiting. But if the doctor tells you that only so can you be rid of something which is poisoning you and you believe him then, unless you want death most of all, you will take it. That is what believing the doctor means.

The trouble is that you can never be sure what you most want to do until you do it. That is why at the present moment it means nothing to say, "I know I can do Y rather than X". The most you can say is, "I think I can do Y rather than X" Nor can anyone else decide the matter for you.

The doctor may tell you that you are physically capable of Y, but that is not the point. The brain surgeon may take a scan and say, "What you really want is to do Y". The moralist may tell you, "What you really ought to do is Y". But if either does so he has altered the whole situation. Now, at this precise moment, I have to decide what to do (if only to put off the decision) and that means doing it. If I tell someone afterwards that I could have done otherwise than I did and she retorts, "Then why didn't you do it?" the only answer I can give is, "Because I didn't want to". And that merely shows that I wanted to do X more than Y – and that it was that wanting that made Y impossible. (The only other answer, "I don't know why I did it," leaves both the speaker and the person spoken to with no explanation at all. And if this is the true state of the case – if our choices are free only when they have no cause whatever – then every instance of free choice is a miracle, an event 'caused by God'. Either that or the assumption on which the whole cosmological argument rests, namely that every event has a cause, must be abandoned.)

But if this is so, if "I know I could have done otherwise" is meaningless, what becomes of moral responsibility? The answer must surely be that responsibility is a term which we can only apply with certainty to *future* acts. We *can* answer for past acts but our answer will always take one of two forms. Either "I knew it was wrong but I needed the money." In other words I wanted the money more than I wanted to do what was right. Or else "I would have liked to spend the afternoon at home but I knew I ought to visit my elderly relative in hospital." In other words I wanted to do what I ought more than I wanted to read the Sunday papers. What we have to regret about the past and try to amend is not so much what we *did* as what we *were* – what it was that made us do it. And this means that our future wants will include wanting to become something other than we are.

Of course it is still possible to *believe* that we could have done otherwise. No-one can convince us by mere argument of the necessity of all our choices. Maybe that is the one thing we really can choose: to believe that believing is free, even if nothing else is. And if we can choose between believing that there is such a thing as choice and that there isn't it seems perverse to choose the latter. That would be to say in effect, "I choose to believe that there is no such thing as choice (except in this respect)". It isn't illogical to say that of course, but it is certainly odd.

But then again perhaps we can't really choose even this belief; perhaps we just *find* ourselves believing it – or not as the case may be.

8. All in the mind?

Here are two riddles for you. Can we reason about reason? In other words is there any reason *for* reason, any explanation of it? And can we say what saying is? The two questions are connected, of course. When we reason we do so in words: we talk, in the first instance at any rate, to ourselves. And when we talk we must do so in a reasonable manner if we are to be understood.

The questions are also connected by the fact that they both invite us to search for *terms*, end-words with which the explanations (or are they just descriptions?) of speech and reason will come to a full stop. They are both forms of the questions about the lever and the fulcrum with which Chapter 1 ended and to which I now want to return. Because if these questions cannot be answered we shall have to rest content with some kind of demonstration: "*This* is what reason is; *this* is the way speech works." We may even have to fall back on the idea of enlightenment: "Either you can *see* what reason is or you cannot".

But let's start with what at first sight seems an easier question. Why did people ever begin to believe in God as the source of reason and explanation – as some still do? The short answer is the one in my chapter heading: "It's all in the mind." In other words there must have been a psychological 'cause'. Maybe it was fear of natural phenomena, the seasons and the weather which were felt to be beyond human understanding and therefore in need of a divine explanation. Maybe it was fear of the divisive tendencies within the human mind itself which, if not restrained by divine command, might lead to the destruction of personality or the disintegration of the tribe. Or was it all down to sex? In itself a creative and unifying impulse but one which if not contained could lead to lethal jealousy and competition. There are almost as many theories of the origins of religion as there are anthropologists to propound them. But most are too simple, for at least two reasons.

First of all, why, if there is just one explanation of religion, has it developed in so many different forms? Buddhism and Shintoism, for example, know nothing of a creator and differ profoundly from each other as well as from Western religion. More seriously, even if we could pin-point the emotional and intellectual need which underlies each and every form of faith, what light would this throw on the question of whether or not what was believed was true? That, surely, is something that has to be established independently of the motive for believing it. I can believe that a certain horse will win the Derby on relatively good grounds (information from the stables) or on relatively bad ones (a tip from a friend of a friend). But what makes the belief probable or otherwise is the horse's actual performance prior to the race. Wanting something to be true or fearing that it is not makes it neither more nor less likely to be so.

But there is another point. One religion, that of the ancient Israelites, differs from all those that are not derived from it in a way quite different from those in which they differ from each other. It condemned as the greatest of all evils *idolatry,* the worship of that which human beings have themselves created. And this condemnation included not just images of wood and metal but the products of the human imagination of whatever form, 'concepts' (things conceived) not least. The Israelite prophets insisted that Israel's God was not a member of a class of divine beings, albeit the only member. He was not a member of any class. His name, "I AM", was not a device for identifying him, picking him out from amongst other things. As creator of all that merely is, 'amongst other things' was precisely what he was *not*. God, it was implied, is not an object to be talked about or referred to. He is someone or something to be aware of. And awareness of him ought to be the precondition, in logic as well as in fact, of our being conscious of the lasting existence of anything at all.

Everything, and in particular the events of their own history, could only be understood by the Israelites in this context. Their freedom from slavery, their national self-consciousness and, in due course, the self-consciousness of the individual Jew were all the result of divine acts. And these acts were, like the miracles referred to in Chapter 6, *pointers*. They pointed not only to the origin of Israel as a nation but also to its destiny. And therefore to its responsibility for what lay between. And such events were echoed in the utterances of the prophets by which God was supposed to explain to his people both what he had done and what he would do.

The situation has not changed. For the theist self-consciousness is something *given*. And if the power of speech goes hand in hand with self-consciousness then the power of speech – and with speech, reason – is something given, too. Believing that the world is created means believing that one's *self* is created, whatever that self is. But isn't that just another way of saying that there is no explanation of self-consciousness: you either know what it is or you don't? Not exactly. What it does mean is that language which refers to self is an extension of language which leaves self out. It involves the use of words which are not just symbols, devices to represent things. It involves words which point not to some *thing* but in some *direction*.

The use of such words is not uncommon. 'There' points to another place – anywhere but 'here'; 'then' to another time – anytime but 'now'; and 'you' to another person, anyone but 'I'. These contrasts – between here and there, now and then, I and you – suggest the end-words which we have been looking for:

space, time and *consciousness*. To these three contrasts the believer will of course add the contrast between the universe and God. But perhaps this is the point at which to say something about the first three.

Space is what which is taken up with objects, time with events and consciousness with minds. (Always assuming that there are minds other than my own and not just brains!) The order in which I have listed them suggests both a logical and moral relationship. We can explain events as changing relationships in space between objects; the movement of the planets is an obvious example. It is not so easy to explain objects in terms of events, though modern scientific understanding makes it rather easier.

We can also give an account of consciousness as the ordering of a particular class of events, namely mental events. Such events include: the *labelling* and *storing* of the images of experience, that is to say *remembering* events and the pain or pleasure associated with them in a systematic way; the *retention* of a selection of such images in immediate awareness (we must remain conscious of the beginning of a sentence at least until we reach the end of it); the *re-orientation* of these images in different patterns of association – what would normally be called *imagination*; and of course the *expression* of the effects of our imagination in speech and other forms of behaviour. There is much, much more to it than this but these five capabilities at least seem to be required in anything that can be called a mind.

And this ordering of our minds is permanent in the sense that we can reproduce our experience of the world at whatever time and in whatever sequence we please. We have more control over our minds than we have over other things of which we are aware since the latter come to us in their own order. And we have more control over our experiences than over the objects of our experience, most of which we cannot modify in any way. It is for this reason that we have little responsibility for the world being what it is – coloured, for example; we have rather more for the way we respond to it, for example what we give our attention to; and most of all for the way we interpret it – the way we see it going and the way we want it to go – for example towards a more or less justly ordered society.

What is true of the world is true of self. Consciousness of self comes to us unbidden. We can of course try to rid ourselves of it – by sleep, by self-intoxication or by the cultivation of altered states of consciousness (the rapture of so-called mystical experience, for instance). And it is consciousness of self rather than speech which distinguishes us from the animals.

It is self-consciousness, too, which enables us to imagine a variety of possible futures for ourselves, another capacity which we cannot confidently ascribe to animals. Such possible futures, each with its pleasure-pain measure, we can simultaneously ponder and, in theory at least, choose between. In other words we can ask ourselves the question, "What shall I do?" or more significantly, "What ought I to do?"

Now, as I said in the last chapter, the answer to these questions may be determined for us. The reasons advanced for doing X rather than Y may be mere rationalisations, reasons invented to justify the 'choice' of what is in truth merely preferred. But the fact that there is even an inclination to justify our actions should make us prick up our ears. Why should "I ought to do it" be felt to have any weight at all as a motive for action, whether by ourselves or others? Is this just a man-made device for deceiving others, and perhaps ourselves, about our real motives? Or is there in reason itself, the very process by which evidence and argument are assessed, a means of arriving at a 'right' choice?

At this point we reach a great divide. That, namely which separates those who advocate an 'ought' based solely on argument, a moral law which would apply in any world inhabited by beings *capable* of argument, from those who want an assessment of evidence as well as argument, a moral law for the particular world inhabited by *us*, with all our peculiar instincts and desires. Put very crudely it is the divide between those who say that morality is a matter of how minds must work if they are to be minds at all and those who say that it depends on how human brains happen to work, having evolved as they have. (But could they have evolved differently? Could there, for example, be a race of aliens whose foresight was so much better than their memory that they interpreted the question, 'Why did that happen?' to mean 'What will ensue from that?' rather than 'What caused that?' Or a people whose language contained no words for 'any', 'all' or 'some'?)

Can this divide be bridged? I am not sure. But just for fun, and to try and see whether there might be a way, imagine the following scenario. The time is a remote future. It is a future in which God is never mentioned – not, at any rate, in polite society – but in which an increasing number of people seem to be motivated by a love of reason and a desire for truth. 'Do as you would be done by' is widely accepted as the basis for individual morality. A world government has been established which is well respected. (Don't ask me why.) And the problems of over-population and the equitable distribution of resources are well on the way to being resolved. More and more people are satisfied with what they have.

Into this semi-paradise steps a New Moralist. He announces that there is another more comprehensive law of human behaviour than either that of nature or reason. Neither 'maximise happiness' nor 'do as you would be done by' satisfies him. His prescription is, 'Abandon all prejudice in favour of yourself'. This prescription, he says, is to apply to the collective – the family, the nation and the race – as well as to the individual. And it is to outweigh all other considerations – of happiness, prudence or of honour. It goes without saying that if acted upon it would do away not only with prejudice for oneself but also with prejudice against others. (It would not of course preclude self-care or family responsibility. To abandon either of those is to create a burden for others which we are not willing to bear ourselves.)

Now such a demand is plainly unnatural. When two motorists are involved in a collision we expect each to maintain his own claim to innocence, albeit calmly. The survival of families and nations are put at risk if their members do not offer one another mutual support.

But is the New Moralist's demand *unreasonable?* How does it compare with 'Do as you would be done by' – a prescription which, it is claimed, derives from reason alone? It is similar in being universal, applying equally to all people in all situations. And it is similar in being unconditional; it does not depend on any choice of ends. But unlike 'Do as you would be done by' it concerns itself not with actions but with motives. You should want whatever reason or nature tells you is truly desirable but you should want it for yourself only in the manner and to the extent that you want it for others.

The New Moralist claims that his prescription is more comprehensive than those of nature or reason because it includes both. If nature suggests, for example, that love of freedom is an aspiration proper to human nature then the New Morality requires you to love your neighbour's freedom as much as your own.

What is more this prescription includes 'Do as you would be done by' because it requires it. For 'Do as you would be done by' is, supposedly, a deliverance of reason and reason requires you to make the same assumptions in regard to others as in regard to yourself. Reason just *is* the setting aside of prejudice in the sphere of the intellect. But reason itself cannot commend this prescription. Rather, reason is commended by it. "So on what grounds", the New Moralist may be asked, "is this prescription commended?" And as you have no doubt guessed his answer is, "It is not commended; it is commanded."

The fact that such a command can never be wholly obeyed,

if only because it seems likely that some of our motives are likely to be for ever hidden from us, is not felt by him to constitute any kind of objection. The object of the command is to redirect our mental energies towards an examination of our motives for action rather than the actions themselves.

By means of this prescription in other words, we are faced with a claim: a claim like all others to be ignored, rejected or accepted, in whole or in part. And a claim made on behalf of a creator whose authority (authorship) must be taken for granted and whose ends cannot be discovered, only disclosed. Such, the new Moralist affirms, is the nature of creativity.

Now the object of this digression is not to urge such a claim upon you, the reader; that would require a different book altogether. Only to raise the question whether either evidence or argument or a combination of the two is ever going to be enough to deliver a morality which will command universal assent. Some motive for such a morality there will no doubt be. But why should it suffice to overwhelm the natural and short-term interest with which it has to compete? People can learn to save for their own future, their children's future, even their grand-children's future. But for the future of the human race? A thousand generations must elapse before I can hope to become an ancestor of all humankind.

The question is whether a faith which goes beyond the demands of evidence and argument, while allowing full scope to both, can offer a way out of this impasse. Such a faith involves first of all faith in myself and my willingness to take responsibility for my own actions, whether they have any prior determination or not. Give a child a dog for Christmas. From the moment the kennel is unwrapped, the muzzle removed and the dog free it is the child's *gift*. But only when the child has the confidence to control it does it become the child's *dog*. It is the same with me and my mind. It is only when I see my mind as something *given*, rather than mere fact, that I can believe that I am a free agent; that my responsibility for myself is something that I can accept or decline and not just something thrust on me by nature in order to enhance my self-esteem. Such self-possession will not be acquired in a moment, complete. It will be the result of growth.

Secondly, this faith will involve a faith in other minds. Not just their bare existence – as you might believe in the existence of a planet too small to see but whose influence on other planets could be measured. Other minds, if I really believe in them, will exist *for me*: and I will exist for them. We shall be equal creatures not in some numerical sense, as the economist or statistician sees us, but in the moral sense, neither taking preference over the other in the eyes of God.

Finally, such faith will include a faith in the future of humanity. That this implies the supremacy of reason over instinct and experience over wishful thinking goes without saying. But it implies something more, namely a profound knowledge of ourselves as created beings. The basic explication of faith in a creator is the simple affirmation, "I am Another's". And its immediate corollary is, "So are you." Those two statements, fully understood, completely transform the relationship between us.

Go back for a moment to the New Moralist. If challenged to suggest any reason for obeying his prescription he might reply, "Try it. You will soon find that it answers a need you did not know you had". Mowgli, in Rudyard Kipling's story, was a boy brought up in the jungle by a pack of wolves. Is it possible to imagine such a being surviving? He would not be conscious of hunger for human companionship, never having known it. But were it to be offered he might well recognise it as meeting a need more profound than any other that he *had* known. The offer itself, being unprecedented, might seem 'miraculous'. So also, in the moment of its offer, might faith in God.

9. Life after death

Suppose you believe that what ought to be will be. That one day everyone will say what they mean, keep their promises, have the courage of their convictions. When will this happen? In your lifetime? In anybody's lifetime? And how long can it be expected to last? It seems likely that one day the universe will run down or become so cold that life will be unsustainable. Is that part of what ought to be?

In answer to those questions some people appeal to the idea of life after death. But what does this mean? Since by definition we can have no first-hand experience of it and since, unless we believe in Spiritualism, no-one can verify it to us it seems to be no more than an idle speculation. It diverts our interest from present wrongs to be righted and present ills to be cured. And even if some evidence for it were available how many people would change their lifestyle if they found themselves accepting such a belief? Isn't it just a cop-out for those who see no response to the problem of evil except to wring their hands?

It is of course quite possible to believe in God and not to believe in life after death. To believe that one's life is owed to its creator and obedience due to him despite the fact that it may end at any moment and obedience is linked to no reward. In the Bible the prophet Job is represented as saying, "Though God slay me, yet will I trust him!" But few people are as high-minded as that. And it is just this fact, an objector might say, that makes belief in life after death so appealing, particularly to those who see in religion a means of rendering the masses more docile than they might otherwise be.

Leaving aside the question of reward, the main thrust of this belief seems to be to suggest that the universe was not created for its own sake. The history of the world is not, as one Shakespearean character suggests, "a tale told by an idiot . . . signifying nothing". It is on the contrary a tale told to us, like those we heard at our mothers' knees, to prepare us for a state of affairs of which at present we can know nothing. In the case of the fairy-tale an idealised version of adult life: "they all lived happily ever after." In this case a similarly idealised version of human destiny.

But if we don't know in any detail what it is we are supposed to believe in surely there is no point in even thinking about it? Not necessarily. After all, knowledge itself, apart from the knowledge of our own minds, may be a will o' the wisp. Very strong conviction may be as far as we can get even in regard to such matters as the regularity of nature. So let us see what, if anything, can be made of this belief even though in practice it is often quite a weak one – no stronger certainly than the child's belief that he will one day 'grow up'.

It usually takes one of two quite distinct forms. Firstly there is universal immortality. This is the idea that we all have a mind or 'soul' which can and does continue to exist in some form without an associated body – a mind that can function without a brain. Now it is obvious that none of us has experience of any such thing – at least in regard to minds other than our own. If someone decides to blow his brains out we don't expect any longer to have knowledge of his mind. In the world of time and space – the only world which most people claim to be able to get at – that mind no longer exists.

But of course if you believe in God 'existence' is not confined to existence in time and space. And is it inconceivable that our minds should exist but not in time and space – or at any rate not in space? Suppose you were to return to consciousness one morning deprived of all your senses – sight, hearing, touch, taste and smell. And all those sensations derived from your body – itches, aches, heat and cold. Could you nevertheless be left with something – with memory, imagination, thought and wish? No doubt such an experience would be terrifying past description. But this or something like it is presumably what those people have in mind who believe in the disembodied soul.

Can we make sense of this idea? Are we supposed in such a state of being to enjoy – or endure – any sensations at all? Of time passing, for example? Of our minds wandering? Of boredom or excitement? Can we communicate with other souls? If so, by what means?

Think of one capacity which it seems we must have if we are to continue to be ourselves: memory. As normally understood it is of the essence of memory that we do not remember all that we can remember at one and the same time. If we did it wouldn't be memory; it would be immediate and unalterable experience. In other words we have to get memories *from* somewhere. What we are conscious of, ourselves, and what we can be conscious of, our memories, are two distinct things. And this is a distinction in time and perhaps in space. At one moment we remember one thing and at the next moment another; and we recognise the same self at work in both cases. But the second memory must be somewhere while we are remembering the first. If it wasn't there would be nowhere to recall it from. It seems as though even the disembodied soul must exist in some kind of time and space – or else have all its memories present to it at the same time. Either that or no memories at all.

The second form of life after death is thought of as the result of re-creation or resurrection. Since God can create, it is suggested, he must be able to re-create. And at some future date he will. The re-creation of consciousness when we awake from sleep is supposed to provide an analogy for this, more thoroughgoing, re-creation. The personality, whatever that may be, will once again exist with all its faculties of recognition, communication and so on, but with a different kind of body to provide them. This body, because it is to last 'for ever', will have no need of nourishment or renewal and no liability to decay. Same mind, different body.

But where is this supposed to take place? And what is this new personality which is both identifiable with the old – otherwise it would not be its *re*-creation – and yet, in regard to its associated body, distinct from it? Perhaps we could attempt an answer in terms of the idea of relationship. People in love are often supposed to say things like "This is something bigger than both of us". By that I suppose they mean that the relationship of which they are both aware is something distinct from either partner and yet something responsible, at least in part, for each partner being what he or she is. It isn't just that A, by loving B, makes of B something more than he was before and vice versa. Something, it is implied, has come into existence which wasn't there before and in which both have a share.

And this sense of each partner being part of something which is more than the sum of its parts isn't something which only lovers know about. When a person loses a limb or a family loses a member that person is – and yet is not – the person he was before. And when a family gains a member the same is true. Life after death, the suggestion is, is like becoming a member of a family all over again except that the relationships are already there, ready-made, to be entered into. And the new personality is just the sum of all the relationships in which it participates. But how in that case are we to suppose the relationships themselves to have been created?

The most obvious example of something that can create and destroy relationships is language. Particularly if we allow the word 'language' to include all forms of communication. A mother can and does form a relationship with her child long before the child learns to speak, by means of body language.

At this stage the relationship, because it cannot be acknowledged in words, is often thought of as irrational. (Of course the mother can speak of the relationship to a third person but she is then speaking of the relationship as she perceives it. The 'something bigger than both of them' which I am trying to explain is something more than just what she perceives.) When mother and child begin to speak to one another the relationship takes on a new form: it is acknowledged on both sides as being personal in a more profound sense. We are to think of the relationships developed in the state described as life after death as being more profound still. Human personality as well as being formed by father, mother and society generally is, according to the believer, something created by God. (This is the alternative account of it.) As such it can be dissolved and re-created by him in a more lasting form.

It is relationships, in other words, which give people their identity as persons. "The man with grey hair by the door" might be used to identify a waxwork. (Though even in this case there is a relationship of some kind involved, "by the door".) But "A's son, B's husband and C's father" identifies X beyond doubt as a person and enables us to understand what 'X' stands for with much greater certainty than a description of the former kind. 'X' was, as a matter of historical fact, first used in the context either of the relationship between an infant and its parents or of the relationship between that same infant and the State. (When the birth was registered.)

What is more, relationships enable us to identify ourselves. I know who and what I am largely because I know myself to be A's son etc. And knowing what it is to be a son and a father I know at least something of what I am not only to myself but to my father and my son. These relationships, that is to say, enable me to identify myself both subjectively (as one who enters into relationships with others) and objectively (as one with whom others enter into relationships). And in every case – even the last, by analogy – it is language, verbal or non-verbal, which brings the relationship into existence and, in the world of time, enables it to grow. A male parent who never communicates with his offspring may be a progenitor; he is not a father. It is a great mistake to think that objects and their qualities are somehow more real than the relationships into which they enter. The opposite may well be the case.

But there is a third way of looking at all talk of life after death. And that is to regard it as making a different use of language altogether, the language of myth.

A myth is not the same as an analogy. In the language of analogy a single word and perhaps one or two other words associated with it are pressed into a new kind of service. In the case of a myth it is a whole story. A succession of imaginary but supposedly historical events is used to suggest events which are more personal than historical. When Adam and Eve are expelled from Paradise they are supposed to have become aliens, having to live in a hostile environment and in fear rather than trust. Their relationship with God and hence with one another has been spoilt by their choice of self-determination, their wish to do their own thing, and they have lost their spiritual home. The myth of life after death, if it is a myth, suggests that this home can be restored to them. But of course we are still left asking the questions, "How?" and "When?"

To the second of these questions some people would answer, "Only when the individual personality has been rid of its desire to choose its own destiny. It was that which undid Adam in the story; it is that which undoes the human race." It is true that some people who have had to come to terms with their own loss of freedom, perhaps as a result of a long term of imprisonment for political offences, have emerged with apparently new personalities and a willingness to accept other people for what they are which most of the rest of us lack. It remains a question whether such cases do full justice to the myth of Paradise Regained. Whether, even as a myth, the belief in life after death allows us any escape from the natural view that physical extinction is the end to which every individual, and the race as a whole, is necessarily condemned.

Let us try and dig a bit deeper and ask the question, "Is God limited by our understanding of time?" In other words take a closer look at the 'after' in 'life after death'. If time is just one of the parameters imposed on God's creation so that one can regard the universe as created with time but not *in* time, it seems absurd to suggest that it is also a parameter imposed on God's own existence. To take a simple illustration: if an astronaut takes a clock with him on a journey through space and leaves an identical clock with a colleague on earth, when he returns the two clocks will not tell the same time. Which of the two, if either, has kept time with God? More seriously, if God existed prior to the world's creation and God is changeless how could the passage of such time have been measured? The passing of time surely requires a change in *something*? To have an history, relativity tells us, is to have an history in time-and-space. Can 'God' have such an history as that?

The hypothesis that God is timeless – that is what the word 'eternal' means – raises the possibility of another world or worlds altogether, a world with its own space and time quite distinct from ours. Imagine an author writing a novel. At a certain point it becomes unsatisfactory. The characters as he has created them are inconsistent with the climax to which he wishes to lead up. Something has gone wrong with their development and he realises that he can only achieve his purpose by changing the plot. But this involves introducing one or more new characters. He decides to start again but this time in the middle of the story at the point where the new characters are first introduced.

There are now two books in existence, though both only in draft. Both contain for the most part the same characters and cover much the same ground. But the first draft will be destroyed; it will never be given the permanence of publication. It is the second which is the 'real' book.

I ask you to consider this illustration – myth, if you like – in which of course the author and his book stand for God and his creation only to suggest that however hard it may be to imagine such a state of affairs there is no logical inconsistency in supposing the existence of two worlds in both of which the same characters exist but in each of which the characters have no knowledge of their *alter egos;* nor perhaps of the author himself. These are the time-warps of science fiction. And the author's time-warp, if he has one, is different from either.

If he has one. But why suppose that he has? Authors quite often speak of seeing the whole plot of their book 'in a flash'. Analogously we might speak of God's creation of his world or worlds as single, timeless acts. Of course it doesn't seem like that to us. We can only take in the world a bit at a time. But why should God be supposed to put it out in such a grudging fashion? In any case the author's time-frame is going to differ from that of his characters in a way quite different from that in which the time-frame of the two drafts differ from one another. Many of the problems associated with 'free' choice – how, for example, we can choose to do what God knows we are not going to do – disappear if his knowledge is not in fact *fore*-knowledge at all.

Go back for a moment to the story of Adam and Eve. As I said in Chapter 8 the moment they saw themselves as choosers, capable of acting from something 'better' than instinct they forfeited their paradise. The paradise of doing what was right and enjoying what was healthy without knowing that they did so. Doubt, awareness of their own ignorance and finally despair ensued. Every man is now his own Adam and every woman her own Eve. And, so the myth suggests, must remain so for ever.

As an alternative to this end of the story the myth of eternal life emphasises not the shortcomings but the possibilities of human nature. In particular, the possibility of overcoming the limits of rationality, the necessity of having to choose. We cannot imagine what it might be to know what choice is and yet have no choice because obedience to God was overwhelmingly more attractive than any other possibility. But then we cannot remember what is was to act purely from selfish instinct either. And if God can endow nature with order (the laws of nature) and consciousness with rationality (the laws of thought) there seems no reason why he cannot endow freedom with the possibility of willing obedience to himself (the moral law). Order in nature is limited by the existence of randomness. Rationality in consciousness is limited by the existence of appetite. And freedom to obey is very limited by the existence of cultural and social pressures. Nevertheless if, as it seems, there is no moment which may not invite despair, so there is none which entirely denies us the possibility of unfettered enjoyment of the good ('what ought to be'). It is to such enjoyment that we should look forward however close we may be to death.

Death, in fact, is an irrelevance. What a 'future' life offers is the substitution of one identity, one character, for another: a timeless identity for one which is constantly changing in time. Such an identity already exists. It is unlike God in being created; like him in being permanent. And, being timeless, ready to be assumed at any time.

On this view to speak of resurrection as a *future* event is misleading. Or at any rate it says no more than that in a world of time and space our apprehension of our real selves and the real identity of other people is necessarily incomplete. We look forward to it because as temporal beings that is the only way we can look *for* anything. We look *at* the past and the present but not *for* them. Physical death and the decay which often precedes it have not got much to do with the matter; they simply mark the ending of an individual's efforts to create his own identity.

Such a view would of course be easier to accept if the myth were presented to us not as questionable history but as unmistakable fact. But that would mean writing another book.

10. Postscript

A Christian perspective

In his Autobiography the novelist Anthony Trollope recalls how in one of his lesser known works, *Miss Mackenzie*, he tried to write a novel without any love interest – and discovered that this was beyond his powers. I have tried to write a book about the meaning of 'God' without reference to Christ and, as the reader who has followed me thus far will realise, I too have failed. There is no 'view from nowhere', no moral or spiritual standpoint independent of the viewer's own past history. We all choose a fulcrum on which to turn the lever of experience, some means of understanding the deliverances of sense – and not least the sense of worth. Some people choose reason ("it is undeniable . . ."); others common sense ("it is obvious . . ."); still others self ("it seems to me . . ."). But the Christian chooses Christ, the Eternal Wisdom and Creative Word of God ("I believe . . . ").

And as soon as we link 'Christ' with 'God', however that linkage may be envisaged, the whole picture changes. We find that we are no longer much concerned with physics and biology – not even with psychology as an abstract science. We are concerned with *history;* with human nature as it actually presents itself to us, its origin and its destiny. In other words 'God' is to be understood *only* in the context of human life and experience; and that means the experience of human relationships. Such understanding springs not from discovery, still less from invention, but from disclosure. If, moreover, we seek eternal truth in history and only there our engagement with it will be *personal* since we ourselves are part of history. And it will be *risky* since it will stand to be disclosed in the future as well as in the past. History admits of no controlled experiments.

This is not the place to consider the claims of the Christian Gospels to be exact history, nor the rest of the New Testament for that matter. That its books as we have them are close enough to their first editions can perhaps be taken for granted. (Independent research certainly supports such a view.) And if we have in these books a fair picture of what the first two generations of Christians believed that must suffice.

Anyway it is very apparent from a study of them that from its beginning the Christian Church embraced three paradoxes, three apparently self-contradictory propositions. First, and most startlingly, Christians believed that the world as they knew it was coming to an end and being superseded by another; yet everything was going on much as before. Secondly, they believed that the death of Christ – an event which they saw as marking the beginning of the end – was an act of supreme injustice; yet it vindicated God's claim to be supremely just. Finally they believed that Christ was totally human, owing his existence to at least one other person; yet he was also totally divine, owing his existence to no-one. The grounds they adduced for all these beliefs was what they chose to describe as his rising from the dead.

In this postscript I shall try to elucidate these beliefs by examining the assumptions which make them seem so paradoxical. And I shall suggest that if we can resolve them we may also be able to make some further progress in answering the four great questions which have been left only partially answered. How can we speak of 'God' at all? What is implied by saying that he or it exists? In the light of what we know of his alleged creation can we ever suppose that he is good? And in what sense if any can he be said to *do* this or that?

The New Testament writers lived, as we all do, in two worlds: a world of experience and a world of expectation. The difference is that whereas we expect the world of the future to coincide in all essentials with the world of the past (scientific prediction is based on just that expectation) they did not. We expect the sun to rise tomorrow, money to buy goods, friends to remember us and call us by our names. But the first Christians looked forward to a world in which the sun would never rise – and never set either; money would not be needed; and our characters would be so changed that even our best friends would not know who we were. It is not entirely clear how literal their expectation was in the first two respects; they probably did not distinguish the literal from the metaphorical in quite the way that we do. But the last expectation and the most important – that a person's whole character, her nature and her destiny, would change utterly when she came to believe in Christ's resurrection – that belief was unequivocal and universal. And it was warranted by the change which manifestly had occurred in those who claimed to be witnesses of that unrepeatable event. The assumption that most people make, often without pausing to think about it, that our future is determined by our past, that we shall live and die just as our genes and the chance circumstances of our life dictate, the first Christians would have utterly repudiated. No-one, they would have said, could have foreseen the resurrection or its results – except perhaps the prophets who were always reviled and misunderstood. And when it occurred it changed their expectations totally and for ever.

Here it is important to pause and notice that by 'resurrection' they did not mean 'revival'. Not, that is to say, the resumption of a former mode of life, still subject to the usual limitations of being in only one place at one time and liable to decay and death. The resurrection was not a miracle like the multiplication of loaves and fishes when what is at issue is not so much what is supposed to have happened as whether in fact it did so. In the case of resurrection *what* has happened is at least as mysterious as *whether* it has; in fact it is scarcely possible to distinguish the one from the other. The earlier miracles, whatever else they were, were important chiefly as signs of what was yet to come. The resurrection *was* what was to come. It was the end of all things, or at any rate the beginning of the end. What was going to happen in the end, what ought to be, already was. With it, or in it, every possible human hope had been fulfilled. If in some inconceivable manner all the other so-called miracles (with the possible exception of Christ's conception) could be shown to have been fabricated, the Christian faith would not be substantially altered: the creeds, in particular, would not need to be modified in any way. But if the appearances of the risen Christ could be shown to be hallucinations then all grounds for a distinctively Christian faith would disappear, though of course it might still be true.

This is not to say that a single decisive event – the emergence of a body from a tomb, say – *took place*. That would be rather like saying that the Big Bang took place. The whole point of the Big Bang is that there was no place for it to take, no sequence of events for it to slot into. Rather it is a term employed to give the events which ensued a frame of reference, an origin or starting point. Only in that sense does it account for them. (To give an account of anything you must have a starting point and the natural starting point is zero.) And only in that sense does the resurrection account for the sudden release of spiritual energy amongst the first believers, their unbounded confidence and courage in declaring their faith and the astonishingly rapid spread of that faith across the countries of the Eastern Mediterranean. What the Big Bang is to creation, the resurrection is to *recreation:* the recreation in the first place of human nature but in the end, Christians believe, of nature itself.

What is more, the so-called resurrection is intimately linked with the death which is its presupposition. The crucifixion of Christ, the attempt to de-mean God utterly, is seen as being utterly repudiated by the subsequent offer to Christian disciples of participation in an imperishable form of life. This death-and-resurrection creates not merely a new future but a new *kind* of future – and for the whole human race. The phrase 'the future' now takes on a new significance, admitting possibilities hitherto undreamed of.

So much for the paradox of the end of one world and the beginning of another while to all appearances things go on exactly as before. What of the paradox of good and evil themselves, the claim that the crucifixion of Christ is both an act of supreme justice and supreme injustice at one and the same time? Well, the last word in goodness is not a manifestation of power as that is generally understood but of what has hitherto been regarded as weakness – surrender, submission and the acceptance without rancour of complete nonentity. This act of Christ in submitting himself to the abuses of worldly power and in embracing total rejection is interpreted by the believer as an act of supreme generosity, the giving of oneself in the forgiving of others. And just because it is on his side an act of supreme generosity, it is also an act of supreme justice because divine justice is the giving to others not of what they deserve but of what they need. There are many hints in the Gospels that divine generosity and divine justice are one and the same thing, though the point is more explicitly made in the letters of St Paul. Of course to be just and to be generous don't *look* the same. "Go north-west" and "Go north-east" don't look like the same direction. But pursue either course without limit and you will reach the same destination – the North Pole.

Finally, the paradox of humanity and divinity. How can Christ be both man, a creature, and God, the Creator? Does God create himself?

If I say to you, "My favourite swan is white", you can interpret my words in two ways. Either, "you already know what whiteness is and my favourite swan enjoys that property" or else "You already know my favourite swan and that should give you some idea of what whiteness is (particularly if you also know that snow is white and paper is white)". If what I have said in Chapter 2 is right then of course with reference to the divinity of Christ these two intepretaions are equivilant: each implies the other. But let us ignore that possibility for the moment. Which of these two kinds of interpretation, if either, are we going to give to the proposition, 'Christ is God'? Are we really going to say that we already know what divinity is and that Christ has all the attributes? If so we had better look at them again. Omnipotence? If this entails dictatorial power, the power that intervenes or overwhelms, we can see – from his temptations for example – that this is a kind of power which Christ specifically disclaims. The kind of power that the creeds suggest is that of *authority,* the power of an author to bring into being and sustain in being; not the power to do the illogical, inconsistent or absurd. And it is Christ's peculiar power to create a community of faith.

Omniscience? The creeds say nothing about it and if it implies just the ability to forecast the outcome of a lottery we can suppose that Christ would disclaim this also. But if it means the power to see into the human heart, to be aware of its weaknesses and to understand and exploit the possibility of every passing moment, then that does not seem impossible to perfect humanity. Omnipresence? This is precisely what the resurrection is supposed to entail.

But suppose that 'Christ is God' is taken the other way? Suppose it means, 'you have heard of Christ, read about him perhaps. Well, that should give you some idea of what God is, (insofar as you can have any idea of God at all); the being of unimpeachable authority, boundless patience, complete integrity, perfect self-possession. The more so if you believe that the power which sustains the universe is the same power which illuminates the mind of man and leads him to love the truth'. That, I believe, is the way that one should take the proposition 'Christ is God' – as an invitation radically to rethink the use of this uniquely puzzling word.

What then of 'Christ is human'? Are we to take it that we know exactly what 'humanity' entails and that Christ accords with our current understanding of the word? That science can point to the moment when the parents were apes and the offspring human or when the parents will be human and the offspring supermen? The idea that evolution is still continuing is attractive but, as I pointed out in Chapter 4, it is not consistent with the notion that humanity can choose its own future and in fact must do so. It seems far better to take 'Christ is human' as setting a limit beyond which humanity cannot go – and allow that all other humans fall short of it. We all suffer in some degree from aesthetic blindness, moral deafness or emotional paralysis. (Does anyone know what it is like to be *completely* sane?). If these two suggestions are adopted I do not believe that there need be any inconsistency between 'Christ is human' and 'Christ is God'.

For two hundred and fifty years the assumptions underlying Newton's laws of motion went unchallenged and speeds were added just like anything else. (Someone walking forward at three miles an hour in a train travelling at sixty miles an hour was travelling at sixty three miles and hour.) Then the shocking notion occurred to Einstein that the speed of light might be limiting – that nothing could exceed it – and the Special Theory of Relativity was born. New ground rules were introduced and phenomena hitherto inexplicable were brought into account. The notion that human nature, too, is limited and that all that can be discerned of God can be discerned within a single human life is for many people equally shocking. We can so easily *conceive* of power, wisdom and authority greater than human power, wisdom and authority – just as we can *conceive* of a body travelling with twice the speed of light. But if we are prepared to suspend the assumptions that underlie our paradoxes: that 'the future' means just 'more of the same'; 'justice' no more than 'treating everyone equally'; 'humanity' as equivalent to 'evolution in its currently most complex form', then I believe we can get a little nearer to the answers to the questions I listed earlier on. And to these I would now add a fifth, namely 'what is faith?' and offer just this answer: 'the willing abandonment of the certainties of disbelief'.

But let us return to the four questions. It is convenient to take the first two together: how can we ever speak of God and what does it mean to say that God exists? Here it may be helpful to recall what I wrote in the Introduction about music, namely that to speak of music is in one sense an impossibility. Because if one could say exactly what music was and what it did there would be no need of music to say it with. Now I would like to change the figure. All of us who are not colour blind agree that the universe is coloured but it is the artist who can best show us the possibilities of colour and give us some guidance if we are serious about *noticing* colour and making its appreciation an essential part of life. It is the same with those who say that the world is created. Those who are most aware of its being so – of the world as sustained by God – are the ones most qualified to enable us to apprehend its possibilities. And for the Christian this means to apprehend Christ. To speak of God is, for the Christian, to speak of Christ. Of Christ himself, of the Father he discloses and of the Spirit he imparts to those who believe in him. The old metaphor of light, source and illumination is not easy to improve upon. Christ's life, death and resurrection are to be regarded as God's final word. And those who look for evidence of God's existence in the remote reaches of space and time are looking in the wrong place.

In the same way to speak of human good and human evil is to speak of the acceptance or rejection of Christ's demands. Nothing else. What ought to be – what will be if faith is justified – is just the reign of Christ in every human heart. Whether on earth or in some putative heaven this and this alone is the coming Kingdom of God.

Of course this understanding of good and evil does not encompass purely natural evil. This seems to be regarded in the Gospels as a relative good if it brings home to us the need to be prepared for humiliation and death: "unless you repent you will all come to the same (unpremeditated) end". And we have seen reason to believe that a world in which no disorder occurs is not consistent with a God both of rationality (so that the natural order is sustained) and of freedom (so that rational beings are not mere automata).

Which brings us to the last of our four questions: in what sense, if any, can God be said to do this or that? If he does everything in general, how can he be said to do anything in particular? If everything that occurs is in some sense 'God's will' how can that also be 'God's will' which I am free either to do or not to do?

In Chapter 7 I suggested that any understanding of moral obligation involves some desire, however faint, to fulfil that obligation. To a person without any faith at all, without any expectation that what ought to be will be, this desire will be no more than the desire to act in accordance with reason. With the believer the case is different. For him what ought to be will be – in the end. And it is for him to bring that end nearer because he wants both for himself and for others a world in which what ought to be is.

For the Christian believer the case is different again. For him what ought to be has been – in the person and work of Christ. And his motive in endeavouring to reproduce that work in his own person is created both by a vision of the future and a recollection of the past; by the bringing of that future and that past into the present in ways which he himself cannot fully understand. This active engagement with past, present and future – with the Christ who was and is and is to come – he describes under the analogy of a personal relationship whilst recognising, as he does so, that he is extending the use of the word 'personal' beyond its normal scope.

Whether rationality alone gives freedom to the human mind and if so whether such freedom is anything more than freedom from impulse and ignorance is a question I cannot pursue further here. But a Christian believer will certainly lay claim to a freedom greater than that, and in particular to a freedom from that prejudice in favour of oneself which is so deeply rooted in human nature.

How much of the freedom which the Christian claims he also enjoys is of course another question altogether.